BARCELONA PRECINCTS

A curated guide to the city's
best shops, eateries, bars
and other hangouts

BARCELONA PRECINCTS

A curated guide to the city's
best shops, eateries, bars
and other hangouts

hardie grant travel

CONTENTS

Want the Precincts travel advice without the hassle of carrying around this book? A free digital download is available once you've purchased a hard copy. See the back page for details.

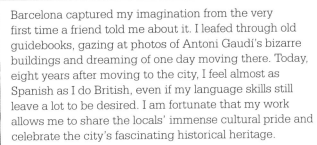

Barcelona captured my imagination from the very first time a friend told me about it. I leafed through old guidebooks, gazing at photos of Antoni Gaudí's bizarre buildings and dreaming of one day moving there. Today, eight years after moving to the city, I feel almost as Spanish as I do British, even if my language skills still leave a lot to be desired. I am fortunate that my work allows me to share the locals' immense cultural pride and celebrate the city's fascinating historical heritage.

Every day I am inspired by the city's rapturous blend of old and new – I love how the Old Town's ancient past is ever present in its labyrinthine backstreets, yet there's always something new on the horizon. From Picasso to Hemingway, Gaudí to Dalí, this sun-struck seducer has played muse to some of the world's greatest artists, yet its thriving contemporary art scene continues to provide a cavalier sense of progress. It's this harmony that characterises Barcelona – a deep respect for what once was, but also for what could be.

This book features the best places to shop, eat and drink in Barcelona's 12 hottest barrios (neighbourhoods). I've tried to include something for all tastes and budgets, and ultimately offer an authentic insight into local life. Whether you want to eat tapas like the fishermen of old or shop like the glitterati, you'll find something within these pages to arouse your curiosity.

This book is packed with places that celebrate the beauty of Barcelona – its food culture, sunny streets, and focus on living the good life – but I encourage you to explore and get lost. Find your own special places and magic moments. This city rewards the curious, embraces wanderers and welcomes the wild at heart.

Ben Holbrook

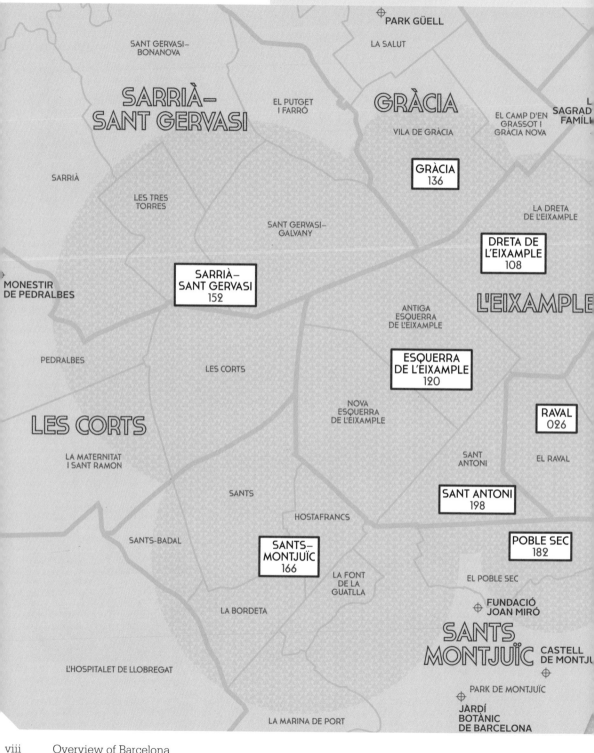

SANT GERVASI–
BONANOVA

PARK GÜELL

LA SALUT

SARRIÀ–
SANT GERVASI

EL PUTGET
I FARRÓ

GRÀCIA

EL CAMP D'EN
GRASSOT I
GRÀCIA NOVA

L
SAGRAD
FAMÍL

VILA DE GRÀCIA

SARRIÀ

**GRÀCIA
136**

LES TRES
TORRES

LA DRETA
DE L'EIXAMPLE

SANT GERVASI–
GALVANY

**DRETA DE
L'EIXAMPLE
108**

MONESTIR
DE PEDRALBES

**SARRIÀ–
SANT GERVASI
152**

ANTIGA
ESQUERRA
DE L'EIXAMPLE

L'EIXAMPLE

PEDRALBES

LES CORTS

**ESQUERRA
DE L'EIXAMPLE
120**

NOVA
ESQUERRA
DE L'EIXAMPLE

**RAVAL
026**

LES CORTS

LA MATERNITAT
I SANT RAMON

SANT
ANTONI

EL RAVAL

SANTS

**SANT ANTONI
198**

HOSTAFRANCS

SANTS-BADAL

**SANTS–
MONTJUÏC
166**

**POBLE SEC
182**

LA FONT
DE LA
GUATLLA

EL POBLE SEC

LA BORDETA

FUNDACIÓ
JOAN MIRÓ

SANTS
MONTJUÏC

CASTELL
DE MONTJU

L'HOSPITALET DE LLOBREGAT

PARK DE MONTJUÏC

JARDÍ
BOTÀNIC
DE BARCELONA

LA MARINA DE PORT

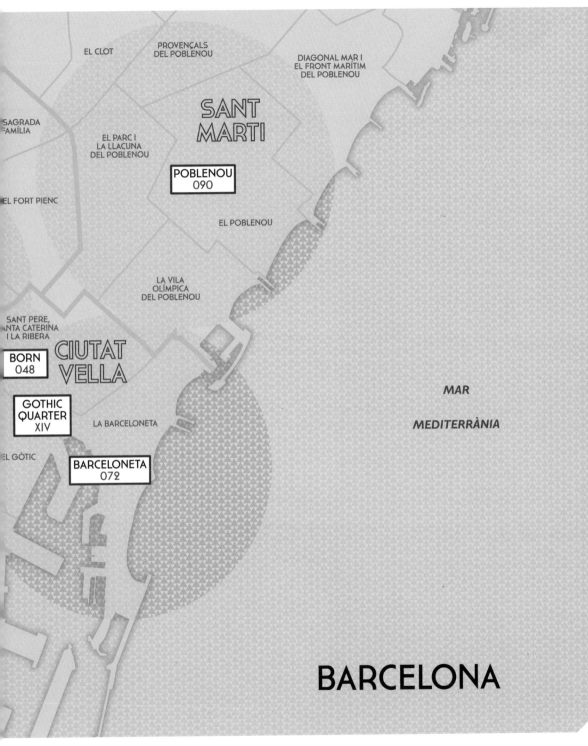

EL CLOT

PROVENÇALS
DEL POBLENOU

DIAGONAL MAR I
EL FRONT MARÍTIM
DEL POBLENOU

SAGRADA
FAMÍLIA

SANT
MARTI

EL PARC I
LA LLACUNA
DEL POBLENOU

POBLENOU
090

EL FORT PIENC

EL POBLENOU

LA VILA
OLÍMPICA
DEL POBLENOU

SANT PERE,
ANTA CATERINA
I LA RIBERA

CIUTAT
VELLA

BORN
048

GOTHIC
QUARTER
XIV

LA BARCELONETA

MAR

MEDITERRÀNIA

EL GÒTIC

BARCELONETA
072

BARCELONA

A PERFECT DAY IN BARCELONA

Barcelona's the kind of city you could dedicate a lifetime to exploring. But if I had only one day here, I know exactly how I would spend it. These are my personal favourite hangouts – a few regular haunts that are well worth working into your itinerary.

I like to explore the iconic (and typically tourist-choked) boulevard of **La Rambla** first thing in the morning, when the stalls are just squeaking into action and the street performers can be seen getting into character. Once the crowds begin to pick up, I dart down one of the many narrow streets that wend their way into the Gothic Quarter. No matter how many times I visit, I always discover new ateliers, restaurants and time-transcending plaças (squares). My favourites are **Plaça de Sant Felip Neri**, with its battle-scarred walls and old (but still functioning) school, and **Plaça Sant Just i Pastor**, with its 14th-century basilica and romantic cafe terraces.

From there, I mosey my way over to the charming neighbourhood of Born. The streets here are wider and sunnier, lined with more sophisticated stores like **Nu Sabates** (*see* p. 050) and **Le Swing** (*see* p. 053). One of my absolute favourite spots is **Plaça de Santa Maria**, where I explore local wines and soak in the views of the 14th-century **Basilica Santa Maria del Mar**. From here it's a gentle jaunt to the **Museu Picasso** or the palm-filled gardens of **Parc de la Ciutadella**.

Midday is when the locals head out to meet friends for a sociable pre-lunch drink or to *fer el vermut* (do

the vermouth), as they say. I enjoy mine at **Bodega Maestrazgo** (*see* p. 060), which is, in my humble opinion, one of the finest wine bars in Spain. After a couple of vermouths and nibbles, I'm always ready for tapas. One of my go-to places is **Bar del Pla** (*see* p. 064), followed by my beloved **Eldiset** (*see* p. 065) to enjoy more tapas and a few Catalan wines. If I crave ice-cream after lunch (I normally do), then I head to **Swiit** (*see* p. 012). Their coffee is great, too, and the little peaceful square out front is the ideal place to enjoy a sweet treat. My perfect day wouldn't be complete without a visit to **Sagrada Família**, Antoni Gaudí's colossal and infamously unfinished church, to check on its progress.

As the afternoon shifts into evening, I like to head down to Barceloneta for a drink by the beach at **Salt Beach Club** (*see* p. 082), which boasts sweeping vistas across the sands. I like to take my paddleboard out for a gentle cruise around the bay in front of the W Hotel.

At around 8pm, it's time for pre-dinner drinks. I'm a regular at **Barna Brew** (*see* p. 210) craft beer bar on ultra-trendy Carrer del Parlament in Sant Antoni and am a big fan of their Belgian-Catalan hybrid beers.

If this was my last dinner in Barcelona, then it would simply have to be at **Disfrutar** (*see* p. 126) for contemporary Catalan cuisine, followed by a few late-night cocktails at **Boadas Cocktails** (*see* p. 044) and live funk music at the **Marula Café** (*see* p. 022).

THE FAMOUS FIVE

Park Güell, Gràcia
Antoni Gaudí's otherworldly park offers sweeping vistas over the city and is home to the Gaudí House Museum where the architect lived for almost 20 years.

La Sagrada Família, Dreta de l'Eixample
This colossal church is Barcelona's most emblematic landmark and Antoni Gaudí's most ambitious design project.

Museu Picasso, Born
This spectacular collection of more than 4000 works of art celebrates the formative years of Pablo Picasso and the time he spent in Barcelona.

Magic Fountain, Sants-Montjuïc
An awe-inspiring light, water and music show that takes place in the shadow of the imposing Palau Nacional (National Palace).

La Rambla, Gothic Quarter
Barcelona's most iconic boulevard (called Las Ramblas by locals, as it is actually a sense of ramblas [rambles]), cuts through the heart of the Old Town and is famous for its street performers, artists and flower stalls.

PARKS & GARDENS

Parc de la Ciutadella, Born
Parc de Joan Miró, Esquerra de l'Eixample
Park Güell, Gràcia
Jardi Botànic, Sants-Montjuïc
El Parc del Centro del Poblenou, Poblenou

ARCHITECTURE

Casa Milà (La Pedrera), Dreta de l'Eixample
One of Gaudí's most celebrated works, this sinuous building is a prime example of Barcelona's world-renowned Modernist architecture.

Hospital Santa Creu i Sant Pau, Dreta de l'Eixample
Designed by Lluis Domènech i Montaner, a contemporary (and teacher) of the city's more famous Antoni Gaudí, this colourful hospital is one of Europe's most elegant.

Torre Glòries (Torre Agbar), Poblenou
Designed by French architect Jean Nouvel, this ultra-modern skyscraper is one of the tallest buildings in Barcelona and hosts a nocturnal light show with the 4500 LEDs that adorn its facade.

Santiago Calatrava's Olympic Flame, Sants-Montjuïc
This avant-garde communications tower was built to transmit television coverage of Barcelona's 1992 Olympic Games. Creator Santiago Calatrava designed it to resemble an athlete carrying the Olympic torch.

Casa Vicens, Gràcia
One of the most recent Modernist buildings to be opened to the public, Casa Vicens was Gaudí's very first house-design commission and is said to mark the beginning of the Catalan Modernist movement in Barcelona.

MUSEUMS & THEATRES

Gran Teatre del Liceu, Gothic Quarter
Dating back to 1847, this decadently designed auditorium is one of the world's most prestigious performance venues.

Museu Maritím, Raval
Housed in the royal arsenal of Barcelona, this historic maritime space is dedicated to shipbuilding from the 13th to 18th centuries and features beautiful scaled models and full-size ships.

Centre de Cultura i Memòria, Born
These fascinating archaeological remains date back to 1700 and depict life in Barcelona before and after the siege of 1713–1714.

Palau de la Música, Born
Designed in the Catalan Modernist style by architect Lluís Domènech i Montaner, this is one of the most beautiful and important concert halls in Spain.

Museu d'Historia de Barcelona (MUHBA), Gothic Quarter
A collection of 2000-year-old excavations, this is one of the largest Roman settlements ever discovered in Europe.

ART GALLERIES

Fundació Joan Miró, Sants-Montjuïc
Dedicated to the work of Joan Miró, Barcelona's famous surrealist artist, sculptor and ceramicist, this is a must for modern art lovers.

Museu Nacional d'Art de Catalunya (MNAC), Sants-Montjuïc
Housing a staggering collection of art from the 12th to 20th centuries, this is the ultimate space to delve into the world of Catalan art.

Galeria Toni Tàpies, Dreta de l'Eixample
This avant-garde gallery celebrates the work of Barcelona-born Antoni Tàpies i Puig, one of the most innovative artists of the 20th century.

Museu d'Art Contemporani de Barcelona (MACBA), Raval
A progressive and often mind-bending collection of contemporary art and audiovisual exhibitions from local and international icons.

Museu Europeu d'Art Modern (MEAM), Born
Housed in a Baroque palace, this modern art gallery prioritises figurative art from the 20th and 21st centuries and hosts regular live music concerts.

FESTIVALS

Sónar, Sants-Montjuïc
A three-day electronic dance-music festival held every June at the Fira Montjuïc.

Primavera Sound, Poblenou
Pop, rock and dance acts take to the beachfront stage of the Parc del Forum.

Cruilla, Poblenou
Three days of hip-hop, rock, blues and pop acts held at the outdoor Parc del Forum every July.

Festa Major de Gràcia, Gràcia
Every August, this family-friendly street party takes over Gràcia for a week of live music.

Fiesta de la Mercè, all over the city
Street parties are held every September to celebrate the patron saint of Barcelona.

The Gothic Quarter ('Barri Gòtic' in Catalan) is the oldest part of Barcelona, the cultural and physical heart of the Old Town. It's also the city's most touristy neighbourhood, but there's no denying its Mediterranean charm. Its labyrinthine streets and alleys are jampacked with beautifully preserved Roman, Gothic and Medieval architecture. It's easy to get lost here, which you inevitably will.

La Rambla is the city's most iconic and touristy boulevard. It sprawls out for close to a mile, lined with boutiques, cool restaurants and street performers. The smaller streets and plaças (squares) that branch off it feel like mini time warps to the past. Their live music venues and nightclubs make this one of the city's wildest party spots.

24   JUN 8OT6

SHOP
1 L'Arca
2 Cereria Subirà
3 Sombrerería Obach
4 Toni Pons
5 It Reminds Me Of Something

SHOP, EAT AND DRINK
6 Avinguda del Portal de l'Àngel

SHOP AND EAT
7 La Colmena

EAT
8 Swiit

EAT AND DRINK
9 La Alcoba Azul
10 Bar La Plata
11 Cometa Pla
12 Satan's Coffee Corner
13 Ocaña
14 Zona d'Ombra

DRINK
15 Harlem Jazz Club
16 Sidecar
17 Marula Café

GOTHIC QUARTER

IT REMINDS
ME OF
SOMETHING

SANT PERE,
SANTA CATERINA
I LA RIBERA

AVINGUDA
DEL PORTAL
DE L'ÀNGEL

VIA LAIETANA

AVINGUDA DE FRANCESC CAMBÓ

CARRER DELS SAGRISTANS

VIA LAIETANA

L4

JAUME I

FONT DE
SANTA
ANNA

CARRER DE LA

Gaudí
Exhibition
Center

MUSEU
FREDERIC
MARÈS

Capella de
Santa Àgata

CARRER DELS BOTERS

AVINGUDA

CARRER DE LA PALLA

Casa de
l'Ardiaca

CARRER DELS COMTES

MUSEU D'HISTÒRIA
DE BARCELONA
(MUHBA)

CARRER DEL PI

Palau
Episcopal de
Barcelona

Catedral de la
Santa Creu i
Santa Eulàlia
(Catedral de Barcelona)

CARRER DEL BISBE

CERERIA
SUBIRÀ

LA
COLMENA

CARRER DE LA

PLAÇA
DE SANT
FELIP NERI

TEMPLE
D'AUGUST

JAUME I

Palau
Requesens

L'ARCA

CARRER DE SANT SEVER

CARRER

Museu Moto
Barcelona

Pati dels
Tarongers

PONT
DEL BISBE

CARRER DE
LA LLIBRETERIA

Gran Hotel
Barcino

CAFE DE
L'ACADÈMIA

LA ALCOBA
AZUL

DEL BISBE

Plaça de
Sant
Jaume

CARRER DE LA CIUTAT

TO SWIIT AND
BAR LA PLATA
(SEE MAP LEFT)

ZONA
D'OMBRA

SATAN'S
COFFEE
CORNER

SINEGOGA MAJOR
DE BARCELONA

EL GÒTIC

COMETA
PLA

CARRER DELS BANYS NOUS

SOMBRERERÍA
OBACH

TONI PONS

Hotel
Condal

CARRER DE LA BOQUERIA

CARRER

BAIXADA DE SANT MIQUEL

CARRER

D'ATAÜLF

CARRER DE LA COMTESSA DE SOBRADIEL

CARRER D'EN RAURIC

CARRER DE

CARRER D'EN

CARRER DE LA LLEONA

FERRAN

D'AVINYÓ

Hotel
Catalonia
Avinyó

HARLEM
JAZZ CLUB

TO LICEU
METRO
STATION

LA RAMBLA

L3

SIDECAR

CIUTAT
VELLA

Plaça de
George Orwell

CARRER D'AVINYÓ

CARRER D'EN CARABASSA

Hotel
Roma
Reial

MARULA
CAFÉ

Plaça
Reial

OCAÑA

Orient
Atiram
Hotel

CARRER DELS ESCUDELLERS

CARRER DELS CÒDOLS

0   50 m

N

1.

L'ARCA

Carrer dels Banys Nous, 20
933 02 15 98
larca.es
Open Mon–Sat 11am–2pm &
4.30–8.30pm
Metro: Liceu

Tucked down one of the Gothic Quarter's many winding passageways, L'Arca offers a beautiful selection of high-end vintage women's fashion. The friendly English-speaking team will help you find everything from Japanese kimonos and 1930s flapper dresses to haute couture hats and designer handbags. Lingerie lovers are in for a treat with lavish silk robes and satin corsets inspired by the 19th and mid-20th centuries. Socialites and brides-to-be covet L'Arca's own brand of dresses and wedding gowns, which draw on the store's previous life as a textile factory to create designs full of ethereal elegance. In fact, the tailors at L'Arca were responsible for designing a number of Kate Winslet's dresses for the Hollywood classic film *Titanic*. The prices here aren't exactly budget friendly, but small accessories like hair combs and silk shawls won't break the bank or take up much room in your suitcase.

LOCAL TIP
The Roman ruins of the Temple d'August (Carrer del Paradís, 10) are the oldest surviving remnants of 'Barcino', which is what Emperor Augustus named Barcelona when he founded it more than 2000 years ago.

CERERIA SUBIRÀ

Baixada de la Llibreteria, 7
933 15 26 06
facebook.com/cereriasubira
Open Mon–Fri
9.30am–1.30pm & 4–8pm,
Sat 10am–8pm
Metro: Jaume I

This candle emporium dating back to 1761 is one of Barcelona's oldest and most whimsical shops. Its colourful Baroque decor – complete with intricate carpentry, sweeping staircase and floor-to-ceiling cabinets brimming with little boxes – make it look and feel a bit like a *Harry Potter*-esque wand shop. The friendly staff will guide you through their stellar selection of handcrafted candles, scented sticks and artistic wax sculptures of famous characters from popular culture. The prices are excellent, making it an attractive place to stock up on gifts to take home.

3.

SOMBRERERÍA OBACH

Carrer del Call, 2
933 18 40 94
sombreriaobach.es
Open Mon–Fri 10am–2pm
& 4–8pm, Sat 10am–2pm &
4.30–8pm
Metro: Liceu

Little has changed at this
old-world gem of a hat
shop: opened in 1924, it
is run by third and fourth
generations of the original
family, and the shopping
experience is still driven by
personalised service.

There's something for every
taste, though the stock is
particularly well suited to the
debonair gentleman. Designs
range from Panama hats and
theatrical toreadors (Spanish
bullfighter's hats) to subtler
flat caps, bowlers and berets.
Simply choose a design from
the window display and
a clerk will measure your
head and provide you with
perfectly fitting hats to try.
Prices start at 15€, making
this piece of history both
affordable and charming.

4.

TONI PONS

Carrer de Ferran, 37
933 17 81 93
espadrillesbarcelona.com
Open Mon–Sun 10am–9pm
Metro: Liceu

Since 1946, Señor Antoni
Pons Parramon has been
handcrafting what are
widely admired as the
finest espadrilles in Spain.
Originally worn by mountain
folk in the Catalan Pyrenees,
espadrilles are made of a
natural rope-like material that
ensures they're comfortable,
durable and add a touch
of timeless Mediterranean
style to any summer outfit.
Collections change with
the seasons and come in
many styles, colours and
fabrics. Prices start at 19€,
making this an exceptionally
affordable place to treat your
feet. The most traditional
styles are those with long
laces, which you wrap around
your ankle and tie with a
bow. Be sure to ask a staff
member for a quick lesson on
how to tie them properly.

3.

4.

4.

4.

3.

4.

5.

IT REMINDS ME OF SOMETHING

Carrer dels Sagristans, 9
933 18 60 20
itremindsmeofsomething.com
Open Tues–Wed 11.30am–8pm,
Thurs–Sat 11.30am–8.30pm
Metro: Jaume I

This handsome, quintessential Gothic Quarter stone facade harbours unique treasures made by the city's emerging artists and artisans. It started as a pop-up store, but its popularity spurred owner Rubén López to find a permanent space to share his collection of 'products and objects with authentic stories'. You'll find a curated collection of hand-carved fruit bowls made from olive wood, eco-friendly leather bags, hand-finished jewellery and more. It's a bit like visiting a museum – one where you are encouraged to touch, hold and buy the art. Prices reflect the quality and singularity of the collection, which means it's not exactly budget friendly. But if you're looking for something special to remember your time in Barcelona, this is a good place to look. Rubén maintains a private gallery available to view by appointment only. Ask him nicely and he might just let you in.

LOCAL TIP
Barcelona's iconic
Catedral de la San Creu i
Santa Eulàlia (Catedral de
Barcelona) is just around
the corner on Placita de la
Seu. Grab a cafe terrace
table and enjoy a coffee
while you soak in the views
and ambience.

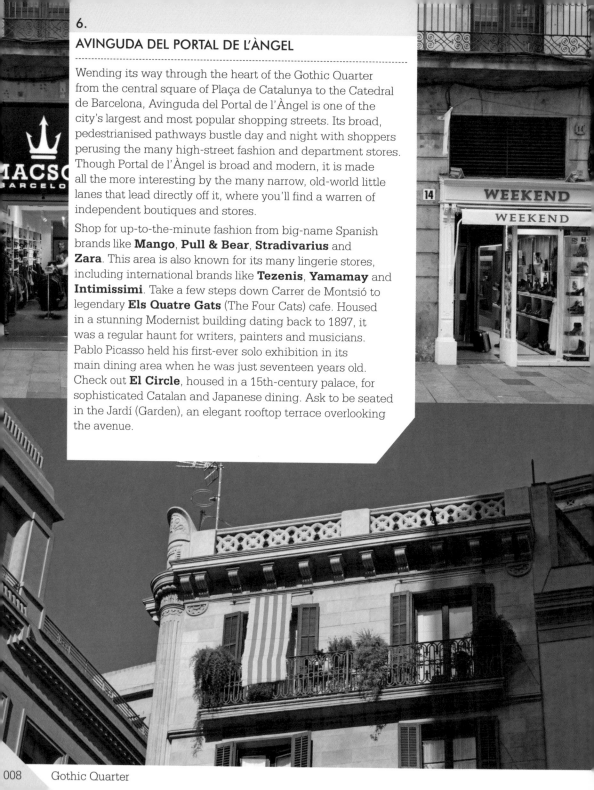

6.

AVINGUDA DEL PORTAL DE L'ÀNGEL

Wending its way through the heart of the Gothic Quarter from the central square of Plaça de Catalunya to the Catedral de Barcelona, Avinguda del Portal de l'Àngel is one of the city's largest and most popular shopping streets. Its broad, pedestrianised pathways bustle day and night with shoppers perusing the many high-street fashion and department stores. Though Portal de l'Àngel is broad and modern, it is made all the more interesting by the many narrow, old-world little lanes that lead directly off it, where you'll find a warren of independent boutiques and stores.

Shop for up-to-the-minute fashion from big-name Spanish brands like **Mango**, **Pull & Bear**, **Stradivarius** and **Zara**. This area is also known for its many lingerie stores, including international brands like **Tezenis**, **Yamamay** and **Intimissimi**. Take a few steps down Carrer de Montsió to legendary **Els Quatre Gats** (The Four Cats) cafe. Housed in a stunning Modernist building dating back to 1897, it was a regular haunt for writers, painters and musicians. Pablo Picasso held his first-ever solo exhibition in its main dining area when he was just seventeen years old. Check out **El Circle**, housed in a 15th-century palace, for sophisticated Catalan and Japanese dining. Ask to be seated in the Jardí (Garden), an elegant rooftop terrace overlooking the avenue.

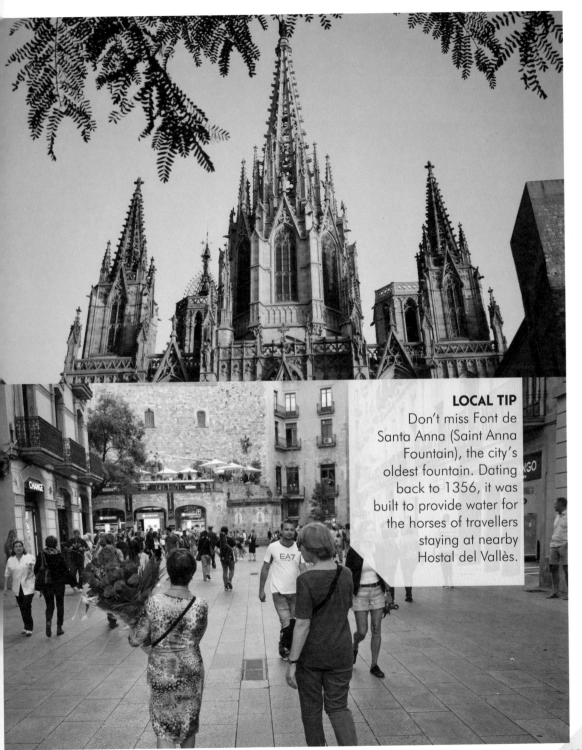

LOCAL TIP
Don't miss Font de Santa Anna (Saint Anna Fountain), the city's oldest fountain. Dating back to 1356, it was built to provide water for the horses of travellers staying at nearby Hostal del Vallès.

7.

LA COLMENA

Plaça de l'Àngel, 12
933 15 13 56
pastisserialacolmena.com/en
Open Mon–Sun 9am–9pm
Metro: Jaume I

It's clear the busy bees at candy store and bakery La Colmena (The Beehive) have learnt a thing or two since opening in 1849. Overlooking charming Plaça de l'Àngel, this shop has a well-preserved history that makes it a beautiful place to wander with a bag of artisanal candy in hand. Treat yourself to traditional Spanish pastries like panellets (sweet almond cakes) and sugar-dusted ensaïmadas (sweet, fluffy pastry buns). Cakes range from classic cheesecakes featuring chocolate, blueberry jam and raisins to contemporary classics like carrot and cinnamon cupcakes with rainbow sprinkles. If you're in Barcelona during the festive season, try one of La Colmena's traditional roscón de reyes cakes, a sort of circular brioche with candied fruit. The pretty box sets filled with chocolates, truffles and Catalan pine-nut panellets make great gifts to take home for friends and family.

LOCAL TIP
Walk down to the Museu Frederic Marès (Plaça Sant Iu, 5), housed in a medieval palace, where you can explore a world-class selection of art, sculptures and curios dating back to the third century.

8.

SWIIT

Baixada de Viladecols, 2c
608 95 16 37
swiitbarcelona.com
Open Tues–Sun 2–8pm
Metro: Jaume I

Housed in an old print workshop in idyllic Plaça Traginers, this artisan helado (ice-cream) parlour offers old-world atmosphere and creamy treats. Husband-and-wife team Gio and Tracy Fontana have been careful to preserve the building's original features, from the scarred stone facade to its antique light fittings. Huge windows overlook the city's old Roman walls, making it a picturesque place to take a break from the Catalan summer heat. Every artisanal scoop is made in small batches by Italian gelato makers using organic milk from Catalan farms, seasonal fruits and natural ingredients. Flavours change weekly and include the likes of creamy coconut, mascarpone and fig, ginger and pear, and dark chocolate sorbet. Gio called on his contacts back in his native Milan to create eight varieties of single-origin coffee, which offers an excuse to linger over an espresso and enjoy the ambience.

LA ALCOBA AZUL

Carrer de Sant Domènec del
Call, 14
933 02 81 41
facebook.com/La-Alcoba-
Azul-170491956318183
Open Sun–Thurs 6pm–2am,
Fri–Sat 6pm–2.30am
Metro: Jaume I

Hidden away in El Call, the historically Jewish part of the Gothic Quarter, this romantic tapas bar is all medieval stone walls, creaky wooden floors and candlelit ambience. There is a range of excellent tapas to choose from, but locals come for the tostas: toasted bread adorned with a range of local ingredients. Try the duck tosta with red cabbage and apple sauce or the marinated mackerel with cherries, basil, garlic and almonds. The wine list features a solid selection of Spanish wines (ask for something from one of the 10 Catalan wine regions) and pleasantly potent gin and tonics. Grab one of the coveted tables outside on the terrace (it's charming, but note you will be charged an additional 15 per cent to sit there) or slip into one of the cosy booths. Stop in around midnight if you're looking for good wine and festive vibes.

10.

BAR LA PLATA

Carrer de la Mercè, 28
933 15 10 09
barlaplata.com
Open Mon–Sat 9am–3.30pm
& 6.30–11pm
Metro: Barceloneta

This tiny, unassuming tapas bar is a local favourite for its simple, traditional dishes. Founded in 1945, it's become quite a hotspot – rockstar chef Anthony Bourdain popped in with his film crew to dig into the specialty house dishes – but it has managed to hold on to its original charm. Unlike most tapas bars in Barcelona, Bar la Plata only offers four options: ensalada de tomate con cebolla y olivas (a zesty tomato salad with onions and olives), montaditos de anchoas (anchovies served on a slice of fresh bread), butifarra (a type of Catalan sausage) and the star dish, pescadito frito (deep-fried sardines – I like to eat them whole, heads, tails and all). If you manage to get one of the six inside tables, then you are one of the lucky few. If not, you'll have plenty of fun eating over one of the wine barrels out front.

Bar la Plata is also a great place to order a traditional wine porrón: a sort of glass bottle with a long spout used to pour vino (wine) directly into your mouth. Watch the locals have a go before attempting it!

COMETA PLA

Carrer del Cometa, 5
646 19 78 45
cometapla.cat
Open Mon 7.30–11pm,
Tues–Sat 1–4pm (lunch) &
7.30–11pm (dinner)
Metro: Jaume I

Cometa Pla is all about market cuisine and biodynamic wines that are healthy and sophisticated – a not-so-common combination in Barcelona. Chef Giuseppe Padula uses organic, seasonal produce to create interesting vegetarian dishes like the signature tatin de cebolla, a playful blend of smooth and salty burrata cream cheese foam contrasted with a crunchy roasted onion. Local meat and fish are showcased too, in dishes like organic braised lamb served over a bed of bulgur wheat and fennel purée, and swordfish tatami with citrus and seaweed. Hidden away on a quiet side street, Cometa Pla has a warm, casual vibe and feels a bit like dining in a wine cellar lined with shelves filled with bottles of organic and biodynamic Spanish wines. The wine list changes regularly, so ask your server to pour you a few varieties to try before you buy.

SATAN'S COFFEE CORNER

Carrer de l'Arc de Sant Ramon del Call, 11
666 22 25 99
satanscoffee.com
Open Mon–Sat 8am–6pm,
Sun 10am–6pm
Metro: Jaume I

In a city suddenly brimming with cool cafes, Satan's Coffee Corner is one of the city's originals – and with its punky skate shop-meets-coworking space vibe, it's still one of Barcelona's hippest. Tucked deep in the Gothic Quarter, it isn't easy to find, but that only makes it feel more like a hidden treasure. Owner and head barista Marcos Bartolomé grinds and blends beans from local companies Right Side Roasters and El Magnifico to create everything from your standard flat white to cold brews and aeropress. Order fresh-cut sandwiches, homemade cakes or pastries if you're feeling peckish.

11.

12.

12.

11.

11.

12.

13.

OCAÑA

Plaça Reial, 13–15
936 76 48 14
ocana.cat
Open Mon–Thurs 5pm–2.30am,
Fri 5pm–3am, Sat 12pm–3am,
Sun 12pm–2.30am
Metro: Liceu

For local liberals, this quirky space in palm-filled Plaça Reial is the place to see and be seen. Named after the fated painter who lived and worked here, anarchist and LGBTQ activist José Pérez Ocaña, this combination restaurant, cocktail bar and club is a taste of the La Movida counterculture movement that swept through Spain after General Francisco Franco died in 1975. It's a meeting point for some of Barcelona's most colourful characters.

The leafy terrace is great for sipping cocktails and people watching, whilst the 1200-square-metre (12,917 square feet) interior is divided into multiple venues: the cafe, which serves traditional Spanish tapas, wine and beer; Ocaña DF, a colourful space serving Mexican and Peruvian-inspired cuisine; and the Apotheke cocktail bar and lounge, whose oriental carpets, ivory pillars and ornate furnishings make it feel a bit like an Arabian palace. Swing by at 10.30pm on a Thursday for live music and upbeat vibes.

LOCAL TIP
Don't miss Plaça Reial's ornate lampposts, which are famous for being Antoni Gaudí's first-ever commissioned design work.

14.

ZONA D'OMBRA

Carrer de Sant Domènec del Call, 12
935 00 58 02
zonadombra.es
Open Sun–Thurs 12–11pm, Fri–Sat 12pm–12am
Metro: Jaume I

At one of Barcelona's cosiest and most charming wine bars, candlelight and a smooth jazz soundtrack set the scene for quiet indulgence. Overlooking the tranquil Placeta de Manuel Ribé in El Call, the Jewish quarter, Zona d'Ombra and its ancient stone walls are covered in shelves filled with more than 300 varieties from every corner of Spain. Miguel Ángel, Zona d'Ombra's affable owner, knows all there is to know about local Catalan wine and is happy to recommend his latest discoveries. Be sure to try a few reds from the rocky Montsant and Priorat wine regions for a taste of what global wine writers are raving about.

Stop in on a weekday for one of the very affordable four-glass tasting flights. Pair your tasting with a selection of sweet Sicilian olives, Cantabrian anchovies and a mixed plate of top-quality Iberian ham, chorizo, salami and sausage.

LOCAL TIP
Just around the corner is Sinegoga Major de Barcelona, Spain's oldest synagogue, which dates back to the 6th century and is one of only five medieval synagogues remaining today.

HARLEM JAZZ CLUB

Carrer de la Comtessa de
Sobradiel, 8
933 10 07 55
harlemjazzclub.es
Open Tues–Sat 8–4.30am
Metro: Jaume I

Music-loving travellers visit Barcelona in search of flamenco, but locals are far more interested in coming to grungy, back-street Harlem Jazz Club to listen to jazz, blues and swing. Harlem Jazz Club is hailed as the oldest live music venue in the city, and it continues to be one of the hottest places to get up close and personal with local bands and solo performers playing everything from rockabilly swing to Cuban cha-cha-cha. If you're in the mood for something traditional, Harlem's performances sometimes feature Catalan rumba, Barcelona's upbeat twist on flamenco. The drinks are reasonably priced, unlike other music venues in the city, and DJs keep the party going well after the musicians have finished their sets.

16.

SIDECAR

Plaça Reial, 7
933 02 15 86
sidecarfactoryclub.com
Open Mon–Thurs 7pm–5am,
Fri–Sat 7pm–6am
Metro: Liceu

Tucked in nightlife hotspot Plaça Reial, Sidecar has been Barcelona's go-to contemporary music venue for more than 30 years. Things get loud and wild on a nightly basis with crowds of local rock 'n' rollers and visiting music lovers. The bargain cocktails are colourful and punchy, but it's the legendary cubatas (whisky, rum or vodka with Coke) that really get the party started. With its suitably irreverent red-and-black colour scheme, the small subterranean stage hosts up-and-coming acts from all across Europe and beyond, with genres ranging from indie rock, punk and pop to soul, funk and folk. It's hot, sticky, and reminds me a lot of the legendary Cavern Club in Liverpool, England, which launched The Beatles to stratospheric heights of stardom.

17.

MARULA CAFÉ

Carrer dels Escudellers, 49
933 18 76 90
marulacafe.com
Open Sun–Thurs 11pm–5am,
Fri–Sat 11.30pm–6am
Metro: Liceu

Hugely popular with the hip, slightly more mature crowd, Marula Café is a safe haven from the sounds of contemporary pop. Located on one of the Gothic Quarter's narrowest and busiest streets, this time warp of a venue is dedicated to the danceable sounds of old-school funk, disco, soul and Afrobeat. Live bands and international DJs pump out infectious grooves and ensure the dance floor is always packed. The vibe is strictly casual and refreshingly unpretentious compared to some of Barcelona's larger clubs. You'll see most people clutching 7€ Heinekens (the least expensive drink on offer), but I suggest splurging on one of the classic cocktails. Arrive before 1am – still early, by Spanish standards – for free or reduced entry.

THE CAPITOL CITY DUSTERS
2003 SPRING EUROPEAN TOUR

Head to bustling Plaça de George Orwell, or La Plaça Tripi (Acid Square) as it's affectionately known, to see the surrealist sculpture and enjoy its eclectic array of watering holes.

16.

16.

Lively **Plaça de Sant Felip Neri** is home to an ancient school whose walls are heavily scarred from the horrific street battles that took place here during the Spanish Civil War. Tranquil **Plaça de Sant Just** harbours the magnificent 13th-century Basilica dels Sants Just i Pastor as well as Barcelona's oldest fountain, which dates back to 1367. Don't miss the weekend farmers' market at **Plaça del Pi** where you can pick up top-quality cured meats, cheeses and seasonal fruits.

Don't miss the big brand boutiques that line **Avinguda del Portal de l'Àngel**. From here, you can jot off down **Carrer del Bisbe**, stopping to take photos of intricate, neo-Gothic **Pont del Bisbe** (Bishop's Bridge).

To learn more about Barcelona's Roman history, swing by the **Museu d'Historia de Barcelona (MUHBA)** (Plaça del Rei, ajuntament.barcelona.cat/museuhistoria/ca) and trace the ancient streets and market stalls that marked the beginning of the city after Emperor Augustus founded it around 10 BCE.

Located at the bottom of La Rambla you'll find the towering **Mirador de Colón (Christopher Columbus Monument)** (Plaça Portal de la Pau), said to mark the spot where Columbus returned to Spain after his first voyage to the Americas. Not many visitors realise there's a small elevator inside the column, which will take you up to a small viewing room that offers sweeping views over the port and city.

Tracy and Giovanni Fontana own Swiit (*see* p. 012), an artisanal ice-cream parlour in the Gothic Quarter.

Puertas Abiertas (Open Doors) I take every chance to see behind some of the area's big doors. We have neighbours who live in a building that was once a hotel, and the interior stairwell looks like something from an Escher drawing. The city often offers puertas abiertas (open door) days when they open up many of the city's palaces to the public. We always try to check out something new.

There is nothing like the street that runs from La Daguería and Plaça Sant down to Plaça Traginers. When we first visited Barcelona years ago, we just loved the atmosphere of this street's old palaces and narrow laneways. What a surprise when we discovered that the old print shop-turned-loft I coveted on the internet, and which we turned into Swiit, was here.

We are at *kilometro zero* when it comes to restaurants; within seconds, we can be at any one of our favourites. There's **Antic Bocoi** (Baixada de Viladecols, 3) for fondue and pan con tomate (bread with tomatoes), **Belmonte** (Carrer de la Mercè, 29) for patatons and goat cheese salad and **Mirilla** (Carrer del Regomir, 16) for Galician octopus. When the weather is nice, it's a treat to sit in Plaça Sant Just at **Cafè de l'Acadèmia** (Carrer dels Lledó, 1).

This vibrant cultural melting pot was once quite seedy – its name, from the Spanish word arrabal (slum), hints at its sordid past. The lurid activity in what was once the city's red light district was a source of fascination to a young Pablo Picasso, who immortalised it in many of his Blue Period paintings. In a bid to free Raval from its reputation, the local government turned it into an artistic and cultural hub.

Raval boasts the diversity brought in by migrant workers during the Industrial Revolution and the creative entrepreneurs who have turned it into a shopping hotspot. It's still a little rough around the edges (be careful where you leave your bag), but you simply can't visit Barcelona without exploring it.

Map labels:

TO MAP RIGHT (VIA CARRER DE L'HOSPITAL)

Hotel Inglés
Hotel Condal
EL GÒTIC
LICEU
Jardins de la Casa Ignacio de Puig
Hotel Moderno BCN
L3
Flor Parks Hotel
SANT PAU
GRAN TEATRE DEL LICEU
LA RAMBLA
CARRER DE FERRAN
ROCAMBOLESC
CARRER DE
FONDA ESPAÑA
LA RAMBLA
Oriente Atiram Hotel
Hotel España
CARRER DE BARBERA
CARRER
EL RAVAL
CARRER DE LES PENEDIDES
Hotel Peninsular
CARRER DEL MARQUÈS
LA RAMBLA
BAR CAÑETE
CARRER NOU DE LA RAMBLA
PALAU GÜELL
MISCELANEA

24   JUN 8976

SHOP
1 Les Topettes
2 Holala! Plaza
3 Discos Revolver
4 Grey Street
5 Fantastik
6 Wilde Sunglasses

EAT
7 Granja M. Viader
8 Rocambolesc

EAT AND DRINK
9 Caravelle
10 Elisabets
11 Bar Cañete
12 Fonda España
13 Ølgod

DRINK
14 Boadas Cocktails

RAVAL

LES TOPETTES

Carrer de Joaquín Costa, 33
935 00 55 64
lestopettes.com
Open Mon 4–9pm, Tues–Sat
11am–2pm & 4–9pm
Metro: Universitat

Journalist Lucía Laurín and interior designer Oriol Montañés have combined their passions for design and personal grooming to create this well-curated shrine to artisanal soap and perfume. Nestled away on eclectic Carrer de Joaquín Costa, Les Topettes brings an independent spirit to Barcelona's otherwise mainstream sea of cosmetics stores. The crisp white space smells like a blooming English garden, adorned with shelves and tables where you can try before you buy. Shop for boutique brands that you'll be hard-pressed to find anywhere else: beautiful bottles of perfume and matching scented candles from Hierbas de Ibiza, luxury lip balms from Juniper Ridge and vegan skin creams from Cowshed. There's an impressive selection for men too, so you're sure to find something no matter whom you're shopping for.

2.

HOLALA! PLAZA

Carrer de Valldonzella, 2
933 02 05 93
holala-ibiza.com
Open Mon–Sat 11am–9pm
Metro: Universitat

Barcelona is famous for its wealth of vintage fashion stores, and Raval is home to the very best – including this one. Established in 1972, this sprawling, multi-storey emporium stocks the highest quality vintage fashion. Raid the racks for everything from sweaters, shirts and shoes to dresses, denim and designer accessories. Don't miss their unique range of authentic military pieces and colourful American baseball jackets. Beyond fashion, Holala!'s passion for vintage style and design has seen them branch out into the world of homewares. Shop for pieces imported from France's Saint Tropez and across the United States. Expect everything from retro dining tables, sofas and lighting to arcade games and surfboards from the '70s and '80s.

3.

DISCOS REVOLVER

Carrer dels Tallers, 13
933 02 16 85
revolverrecords.es
Open Mon–Sat 10am–9pm
Metro: Catalunya

Vinyl may be making a comeback, but stepping into this ultra-cool little record store will make you feel like it never went out of style. Discos Revolver is a must-stop shop for music lovers on narrow, punky Carrer dels Tallers, better known as Barcelona's 'music street', lined with alternative fashion stores and guitar shops. This vanguard of vinyl is a proper old-school record store, full of shelves and crates packed with everything from indie to electronic dance music and grunge to rock'n'roll. But the real showstopper is their collection of records by Spanish indie bands and labels. A hub for the local music scene, Discos Revolver is an excellent place to hear about local gigs and buy discounted tickets.

2.

2.

2.

3.

3.

4.

GREY STREET

Carrer del Peu de la Creu, 25
greystreetbarcelona.com
Open Mon–Sat 11am–3pm &
4–9pm
Metro: Sant Antoni

Grey Street is a colourful
Aladdin's cave full of artsy
gifts and precious items
from local designers and
international artisans. Tucked
away on a quiet side street,
this gorgeous gem of a gift
shop has preserved the
building's original facade,
including a sign that reads
'Novedades Perfumería' – a
nod to the property's previous
incarnation as a perfumerie.
Australian owner and head
curator Amy Cocker stocks
choice items ranging from
luxurious stationery to
contemporary Spanish pottery,
art prints and handcrafted
jewellery, so you'll have no
trouble picking out a unique
souvenir or two from your
time in the Catalan capital
of cool.

LOCAL TIP
Pop around the corner to Lolos (Carrer de la Lluna, 2b) if you're looking for more ultra-cool casualwear from local designers.

5.

FANTASTIK

Carrer de Joaquín Costa, 62
933 01 30 68
fantastik.es
Open Mon–Fri 11am–2pm &
4–8.30pm, Sat 11am–3pm &
4–9pm
Metro: Universitat

This offbeat bazaar full of treasures and trinkets embraces the diversity and unconventional spirit that makes Raval unique. Owner Juanra Ramón traverses the globe in search of curiosities that are colourful, kitsch and downright odd – a perfect fit for a shop in what Juanra calls the 'most multicultural neighbourhood in town'. Browse mystical religious accoutrements, including paintings of Hindu goddesses and fluorescent statues of the Virgin Guadalupe, wind-up toy robots from China and ceramic sugar skulls from Mexico. The selection is vast and varied, but one thing's for sure: you won't find a shop quite like it anywhere else in the city.

LOCAL TIP
While you're here, check out the vintage homewares and furniture at Fusta'm (Carrer de Joaquín Costa, 62).

6

WILDE SUNGLASSES

Carrer de Joaquín Costa, 2
654 45 50 57
wildesunglasses.com
Open Mon–Sat 12–9pm,
Sun 4.30–8.30pm
Metro: Universitat

The city's blissful Catalan rays inspired fashionistas Cao Azuaje (from Venezuela) and Teppei Kikugawa (from Japan) to open their boutique of handcrafted eyewear, where every pair is hand-picked from urban auctions and private collections around the globe. The emphasis here is on rare vintage frames from luxury brands like Yves Saint Laurent, Ray-Ban and Lacoste as well as treasured boutique brands and non-branded beauties. The neon lights, guitar amps and retro boom boxes add a suitably urban flair that makes you feel like you're in an underground music club.

Their early success inspired Cao and Teppei to create their own range of sunglasses, featuring daring designs inspired by frames found in their own enviable collections and the '50s subculture style made popular by the Japanese mafia. No matter what style you choose, you're bound to walk out of Wilde with a fresh perspective.

7.

GRANJA M. VIADER

Carrer d'en Xuclà, 4–6
933 18 34 86
granjaviader.cat
Open Mon–Sat 9am–1.15pm &
5–9.15pm
Metro: Catalunya

Opened in 1870, this well-loved granja (milk bar) is said to be the oldest cafe in Barcelona. Run by the same family for five generations, it feels a bit like a living museum: many of the bow-tied waiters have worked here since they were boys. The decor has remained untouched, with Parisian-style tables and walls clad in crinkly old photos that prove it. They continue to uphold the Spanish tradition of indulging in a sweet breakfast or merienda (afternoon snack). In fact, one of Spain's most iconic confections, the Cacaolat chocolate milkshake, was invented here.

Today, Granja M. Viader is all about the churros con chocolate (pictured at right). These crispy, deep-fried beauties are generously sprinkled with sugar and come with a bowl of treacle-thick hot chocolate for your dunking pleasure. While you're here, be sure to try their mató i miel (a soft cheese with honey and walnuts), a quintessential Catalan dessert.

8.

ROCAMBOLESC

La Rambla, 51–59
680 73 73 97
rocambolesc.com
Open Mon–Thurs 12–11pm,
Fri–Sun 12pm–12am
Metro: Liceu

Jordi Roca was named World's Best Pastry Chef in 2014, so it's hardly surprising that Rocambolesc is far from your average ice-cream parlour. Their bizarre flavour combinations, which include parmesan, asparagus and truffle, and olive oil with toasted bread, work beautifully alongside sweeter flavours like baked apple with shortbread and strawberry with honey rocks and violet marshmallow. The sorbet popsicles are like miniature art sculptures, bursting with flavours like blueberry with vanilla and blood orange with mango. Jordi Roca is one of the three Roca brothers who found fame when their restaurant El Celler de Can Roca was first named Best Restaurant in the World in 2013. Their reputation means these cones are pricier than your average, but this is definitely the most affordable way to have a Roca brother dining experience.

LOCAL TIP

Make sure to have a look around the Gran Teatre del Liceu (La Rambla, 51–59), one of the world's most beautiful opera houses.

8.

7.

7.

9.

CARAVELLE

Carrer del Pintor Fortuny, 31
933 17 98 92
caravelle.es
Open Mon 9.30am–5.30pm,
Tues–Fri 9.30–1am, Sat
10–1am, Sun 10am–5.30pm
Metro: Catalunya

The Spanish are so proud of their cuisine that they were quite happy to eat nothing else until recently, when places like Caravelle appeared on the scene. Everything about this cosy arcadia, from the funky decor to its Mexican-, American- and British-inspired cuisine, is distinctly non-Spanish. Created by Australian-British couple Zim Sutton and Poppy Da Costa, the concept is simple: homemade everything. They do everything in-house, from smoking their own meats to brewing up their own colas and craft beer, offering excellent value for money.

Kickstart your day with a brunch of poached eggs, corn fritters, avocado and pesto, and a specialty coffee made with beans from local roasters Nomad Coffee. The burgers and tacos make for hearty lunch or dinner feasts, especially when paired with a house-brewed beer like the Galactic Pale Ale. If you're into craft beer, be sure to ask Zim for a quick tour of his nanobrewery.

LOCAL TIP
Don't miss nearby Mercat de la Boqueria (La Rambla, 91), founded in 1840 and the city's most famous food market. Get there as early as possible to avoid maddening crowds.

CARAVELLE

31

10.

ELISABETS

Carrer d'Elisabets, 2
933 17 58 26
Open Mon–Thurs 7.30–12am,
Fri 9.30–1am, Sat 9–12am
Metro: Catalunya

Traditional Spanish restaurants aren't about fancy interior design or over-the-top customer service, but generous portions at equally generous prices, which is exactly what Elisabets offers. It may not look like much from the outside – the decor clearly hasn't been touched since it opened in 1962 – but inside, you'll find hordes of regulars hunched over steaming bowls of ragú de jabalí (wild boar stew), sharing raciones (rations, which are bigger than tapas) of pimientos de Padrón (pan-fried peppers) and taking greedy glugs of beer. Don't miss the highly addictive, bite-sized tapas dishes like choricitos (little spicy sausages cooked in cider) and patatas rabiatas (chunky fried potatoes topped with spicy bolognese salsa). 'Cheap and cheerful' has never tasted so good. Grab one of the cosy stained-glass booths out back and order the menú del día (set lunch menu) for a bargain three-course lunch.

11.

BAR CAÑETE

Carrer de la Unió, 17
932 70 34 58
barcanete.com
Open Mon–Sat 1pm–12am
Metro: Liceu

Hidden away on a shabby backstreet just steps from the famous boulevard of La Rambla, this temple of tapas is something of a well-kept secret. Its flamboyant facade, all gold-on-black and dark wood, is a contrast from the neighbouring mobile-phone shops and graffitied walls. The sensory goodness continues inside, where restaurant manager Don Julio commands a crew of white-coated waiters who glide between tables and serve up traditional Catalan tapas and goblets of quality Spanish wine. Bar Cañete isn't fancy, but every dish has some refined twist: traditional potato croquettes (a sort of crisy fried potato ball) are pepped up with chunks of lobster, and the already-toothsome wild tuna tartare with mascarpone is embellished with a decadent dollop of caviar. Cañete is fairly pricey, but the menú del día (set lunch menu) offers superb value for money. Be sure to sit at the long bar so you can catch the action as chefs jostle flaming pans in the open kitchen.

11.

10.

10.

11.

10.

12

FONDA ESPAÑA

Sant Pau, 9–11
935 50 00 10
hotelespanya.com/en/
restaurante-fonda-espana-1
Open Mon–Sat 1–4pm (lunch)
& 8–11pm (dinner), Sun 1–4pm
Metro: Liceu

With a Modernist makeover courtesy of iconic architect Lluis Domènech i Montaner, this sophisticated Catalan restaurant tucked inside the Hotel España is one of the city's most beautiful dining rooms. Executive chef Martín Berasategui also runs Lasarte, Barcelona's only three-Michelin-starred restaurant, while the kitchen is managed by revered chef German Espinosa. There are no Michelin stars here – at least, not yet – making it a fairly affordable place to explore the delights of contemporary Catalan cooking. Splurge on the 17-course Trip Through Modernism tasting menu (75€), which includes flavours like vermouth with citrus and salmon roe, and pigeon with foie gras and hazelnut praline. For fine dining at wallet-friendly prices, go for the lunch menu: at 27€, it's a genuine bargain. Hotel España's glamorous rooftop terrace provides stunning views across the city and is the perfect place to enjoy a post-dinner cocktail.

13.

ØLGOD

Carrer de l'Hospital, 74
934 43 90 82
olgodbcn.com
Open Mon–Sun 3pm–2am
Metro: Liceu

This Danish-owned craft beer bar brings something a little different to Barcelona's local brew-centric beer scene: an interesting selection from all over Europe. You'll find 30 taps behind the minimalist concrete bar pumping out an interesting array from Denmark, Sweden, the UK and Spain. Paintings by local and international artists bring the crisp white walls to life, making it an interesting place to sit and sip. Many of the Scandinavian bartenders speak excellent English, so don't be afraid to ask for a few samples and recommendations. The bargain 15€ tasting flight, which includes five different beers, is a great place to start. The beer cocktails may sound odd, but trust me, the Mexican Michelada (a beery take on the Bloody Mary) is the perfect way to cool off on a hot day or balmy night.

Order something from the smokehouse menu, which features hearty fare like pastrami and smoked brisket sandwiches. There are some solid options for vegetarians too, including smoked seitan salads, sandwiches and burgers.

14.

BOADAS COCKTAILS

Carrer dels Tallers, 1
933 18 95 92
boadascocktails.com
Open Mon–Thurs 12pm–2am,
Fri–Sat 12pm–3am
Metro: Catalunya

This storied watering hole off a particularly touristy strip of La Rambla is the oldest cocktail bar in Barcelona, but its unassuming facade ensures that only the enlightened know it's there. The bar's origins can be traced back to the early 1920s when young Catalan Miguel Boadas moved to Cuba to work at his cousin's bar, El Floridita, immortalised in these words by Ernest Hemingway: 'My mojito at La Bodeguita and my daiquiri in El Floridita'. Miguel returned home and opened his own El Floridita–inspired bar, which quickly became popular with the local glitterati. You're still likely to find yourself bumping shoulders with politicians, artists and media types here. The tiny space is decked out in Art Deco splendour, complete with tuxedoed bartenders who are well versed on the classics and happy to make recommendations. Try the cocktail of the day (it's usually cheaper than everything else) or take Hemingway's word for it and order a daiquiri.

LOCAL TIP

Not far from here is the space-aged Barceló Raval Hotel (Rambla del Raval, 17–21). Take the lift up to the top floor and revel in the 360-degree views across Barcelona's colourful skyline.

13.

14.

Negotiate your way through the thronging crowds to the cultural hub of **Plaça dels Àngels**. Here you'll find avant-garde art at the **Museu d'Art Contemporani de Barcelona (MACBA)** (Plaça dels Àngels, 1, macba.cat/en); arthouse film screenings and vintage camera equipment displays at the **Filmoteca de Catalunya** (Plaça de Salvador Seguí, 1–9, filmoteca.cat/web/en); and temporary art exhibitions at the **Centre de Cultura Contemporània de Barcelona (CCCB)** (Carrer de Montalegre, 5, cccb.org/en).

Small, independent art gallery **Miscelanea** (Carrer de Guàrdia, 10, miscelanea.info/) hosts exhibitions and workshops by local artists. The hidden bar out back is a great place to hang with creative types, and the gift shop is packed with colourful books and art prints by local artists.

Check out the **Teatre del Raval** (Carrer de Sant Antoni Abat, 12, teatredelraval.com), a classic-style theatre specialising in small-format productions.

Pose for a photo under the palm trees that line Rambla del Raval with the iconic **El Gato de Botero** (The Raval Cat), designed by Colombian artist Fernando Botero. On your way back towards the city centre, hunt out Antoni Gaudí's eerie **Palau Güell** (Carrer Nou de la Rambla, 3–5, palauguell.cat/en), one of the architect's lesser-known works.

Rebecca McNally Coleman
is owner of Marmalade Restaurant & Lounge (marmaladebarcelona.com), which has been serving dinner, cocktails and weekend brunch in Raval since 2007.

Oleocteca (Carrer dels Àngels, 20): They offer a wonderful selection of olive oils, along with cosmetics, shampoos, soaps, chocolates and beer all made from or using olive oil. The staff gift-wrap everything so beautifully.

Barceló Raval (Rambla de Raval, 17–21): Take the lift up to the top floor and enjoy the spectacular 360-degree views with a beer on the rooftop terrace.

Café Teatre Llantiol (Carrer de la Riereta, 7): This small theatre deep in the narrow old streets of Raval provides an alternative performing-arts theatre experience. Get a table near the stage and you will feel like you are part of the show.

Antic Hospital de la Santa Creu (Carrer de Hospital, 56): This 15th-century landmark exemplifies Raval's harmonious blend of cultures. It currently houses the city's library and a little outdoor cafe called El Jardin, which is a great place to relax with a book and a coffee.

Kino (Carrer Ferlandina, 23): This cafe's sunny terrace is the perfect spot to while away the afternoon. The skateboarders that gather in the square outside the nearby MACBA museum provide plenty of entertainment.

Casa Almirali (Carrer de Joaquín Costa, 33): Founded in 1860, this is one of the oldest and best preserved bars in Barcelona, full of 19th-century bohemian atmosphere. Try their famous absinthe, if you dare!

Built by and for medieval Barcelona's aristocracy between the 13th and 15th centuries, Born is known for its bohemian-yet-sophisticated vibe. It's a place where wealthy art dealers and old-money socialites lounge on cafe terraces, reading large newspapers and flaunting their impeccable style.

Born's broad streets harbour many exclusive fashion boutiques and culinary hotspots. Many say that leafy Passeig del Born, the precinct's main artery, once hosted jousting tournaments (Born means 'jousting field' in Catalan). Today it's lined with restaurants, wine bars and cool cocktail bars. It's also home to the Santa Maria del Mar church, best viewed from one of the cafe terraces that rest in its shadow.

BORN

24   JUN 8016

SHOP
1 Nu Sabates
2 Ici et Là
3 Coquette
4 Le Swing
5 Natalie Capell Atelier de Moda
6 Ivori
7 La Tercera
8 Oscar H. Grand

SHOP, EAT AND DRINK
9 Carrer del Rec
10 Bodega Maestrazgo

EAT AND DRINK
11 Bodega La Puntual
12 Nap
13 Bar del Pla
14 Eldiset

DRINK
15 Collage Cocktail Bar
16 Antic Teatre
17 Palau Dalmases

BODEGA
MAESTRAZGO

0   50 m

Parc
de la
Ciutadella

CASTELL
DELS TRES
DRAGONS

Hivernacle

CIUTAT
VELLA

N

CARRER DELS METGES

CARDERS

CARRER DEL

PASSEIG DE

COMERÇ

CARRER D'EN TANTARANTANA

CARRER DE LA PRINCESA

PICASSO

Jardins
del Forat de la
Vergonya

ARXIU
FOTOGRÀFIC DE
BARCELONA
(AFB)

CARRER DE LA FUSINA

TO
ICI ET LÀ
(SEE MAP LEFT)

NAP

CARRER DE GOMBAU

CARRER DE FONOLLAR

DELS

CARRER

SANT PERE,
SANTA CATERINA
I LA RIBERA

CARRER DEL REC

LE SWING

BORMUTH

El Born
Centre de
Cultura
i Memòria

CARRER D'EN GIRALT EL PELLISSER

Mercat de
Santa
Caterina

CARRER DE COLOMINES

BAR
DEL PLA

CARRER DE LA PRINCESA

CARRER

MERCAT
PRINCESA

DELS FLASSADERS

CARRER
DEL REC

TO
ANTIC TEATRE
(SEE MAP LEFT)

OSCAR H.
GRAND

MUSEU
PICASSO

MUSEU
DE CULTURES
DEL MÓN

ELDISET

COQUETTE

CARRER DE LA BORJA

MUSEU EUROPEU
D'ART MODERN
(MEAM)

PALAU
DALMASES

EL
XAMPANYET

PASSEIG DEL BORN

NU
SABATES

CARRER DELS BANYS

BODEGA
LA PUNTUAL

COQUETTE

NATALIE
CAPELL
ATELIER
DE MODA

CARRER DEL BROSOLI

VELLS

IVORI

LA
TERCERA

SANTA
MARIA
DEL MAR

JAUME I

CARRER DE

L'ARGENTERIA

Hotel
Suizo

Hotel
Banys
Orientals

L4

CARRER DE MANRESA

CARRER DE LA NAU

CAPUTXES

CARRER D'ESPASERIA

Pla de Palau

Palau
Requesens

VIA LAIETANA

COLLAGE
COCKTAIL
BAR

CAFE DE
L'ACADEMIA

EL GÒTIC

Ilotja
de Mar

1.

NU SABATES

Carrer dels Cotoners, 14
932 68 03 83
nusabates.com
Open Mon–Sat 11am–2pm &
4–8.30pm
Metro: Jaume I

This cosy corner shop is the place to go for carefully handcrafted shoes. Its thoughtfully curated brands and designs include timeless selections from artisans such as Catalan designer Deux Souliers and California's Cydwoq, whose shoes are handmade using Italian leather that is treated with 100 per cent natural dyes. For shoes that will forever remind you of your time in Barcelona, try on a pair from the Evarist Bertran range – they are all designed by store owner Roger Amigó and made with vegetable-tanned leather and cordovan in a small workshop in southern Spain. Styles include everything from cool-but-casual boots and sandals to elegant designs that will add an artisanal touch. They're not cheap, but they'll outlast almost everything else in your shoe rack.

ICI ET LÀ

Pasaje de Sert, 5
932 68 78 43
icietla.com
Open Mon–Fri 10am–2.30pm
& 4–7.30pm
Metro: Urquinaona

- -

Ici et Là ('From Here and There') is a treasure trove of handcrafted homewares made by local artisans. From avant-garde metal coffee tables and desks that look like sinuous art sculptures to upcycled vintage armchairs upholstered with velvet, each piece is unique or limited-edition. If you fall in love with the designs of a particular artisan, speak to the staff and they can arrange for bespoke pieces to be made just for you. If money's no object, then French owner Isabel Dubois will have your order shipped directly to your home. Those hunting for something more budget-friendly can browse the colourful cushion covers, ceramics and other small objects of desire. The store's famous ant sculptures, handmade with a single iron wire, will fit snuggly into your suitcase.

LOCAL TIP
The Museu Europeu d'Art Modern (Carrer de la Barra de Ferro, 5) is a great place to discover contemporary sculpture and paintings, as well as live music performed by local artists.

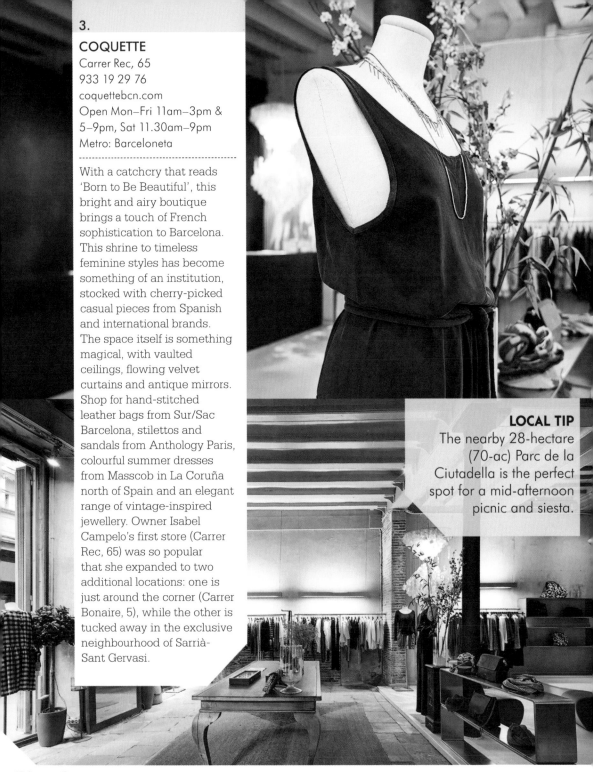

3.

COQUETTE

Carrer Rec, 65
933 19 29 76
coquettebcn.com
Open Mon–Fri 11am–3pm &
5–9pm, Sat 11.30am–9pm
Metro: Barceloneta

With a catchcry that reads 'Born to Be Beautiful', this bright and airy boutique brings a touch of French sophistication to Barcelona. This shrine to timeless feminine styles has become something of an institution, stocked with cherry-picked casual pieces from Spanish and international brands. The space itself is something magical, with vaulted ceilings, flowing velvet curtains and antique mirrors. Shop for hand-stitched leather bags from Sur/Sac Barcelona, stilettos and sandals from Anthology Paris, colourful summer dresses from Masscob in La Coruña north of Spain and an elegant range of vintage-inspired jewellery. Owner Isabel Campelo's first store (Carrer Rec, 65) was so popular that she expanded to two additional locations: one is just around the corner (Carrer Bonaire, 5), while the other is tucked away in the exclusive neighbourhood of Sarrià-Sant Gervasi.

LOCAL TIP
The nearby 28-hectare (70-ac) Parc de la Ciutadella is the perfect spot for a mid-afternoon picnic and siesta.

LE SWING

Carrer del Bonaire, 6
933 02 36 98
leswingvintage.com
Open Mon–Sat 11am–2.30pm
& 5–8.30pm
Metro: Jaume I

This tiny emporium houses an exclusive range of high-end vintage fashion. Big-name brands sourced from auctions in Milan, Paris and Los Angeles run the gamut from Christian Dior and Gucci to Hermès and YSL, with genuine vintage clothing, shoes and accessories for both men and women. This glamorous range attracts an equally glamorous clientele, including Hollywood A-listers Scarlett Johansson and Natalie Portman. Splurge on a 500€ pair of blue leather gloves from Hermès or a 900€ silk-lined Chanel jacket. Gentlemen can choose from a range of pure silk shirts with gold thread and pearl buttons – prices hover around 300€. Browse the glass cabinets for more affordable treasures like jewellery, cufflinks, wallets and sunglasses. Don't miss the little staircase that leads down to another floor of vintage fashion.

5.

NATALIE CAPELL ATELIER DE MODA

Carrer de la Carassa, 2
933 19 92 19
nataliecapell.com
Open Mon–Sat 12–8.30pm
Metro: Jaume I

'Every dress tells a story' at this beautiful atelier, which epitomises the independent spirit that makes Born such a great place to shop. Shopping in the dimly lit space feels like stepping back into the neighbourhood's medieval past, with each item lovingly displayed. Natalie Capell and her team of artisans create delicate garments with hand embroidery and tulle silk fabric made just for her in Italy. Shop for one-off pieces ranging from hand-dyed embroidered scarves to elegant party dresses and ethereal wedding gowns. Natalie organises the occasional private fashion show to showcase their latest designs, so keep an eye on her website for details.

LOCAL TIP
Stroll down to the end of the street and explore the 14th-century Basílica del Santa Maria del Mar (Plaça de Santa Maria, 1), one of the world's largest and most beautiful examples of Catalan Gothic architecture.

5.

IVORI
Carrer dels Mirallers, 7
931 37 02 64
ivoribarcelona.com
Open Mon–Sat 11am–8.30pm
Metro: Jaume I

At this cute fashion boutique, Catalan designer Carola Alexandre curates collections of casual clothing handcrafted in Barcelona by local designers. Housed on a prime corner on one of Born's historic backstreets, Ivori is the place for jumpsuits by Rita Row, tailored trousers by Naguisa and colourful swimwear by Valnud. Carola's Ivori brand features an elegant range of vintage-inspired silk shirts and chunky-knit jumpers. She is also involved in the Climb Barcelona brand, which makes casual menswear inspired by 'mountains and noise'. Prices are reasonable: you can buy an entire outfit for little more than 100€.

5.

6.

7.

LA TERCERA

Carrer del Brosolí 4, local 3
625 30 17 96
namebcn.com
Open Mon–Sat 11am–8.30pm
Metro: Jaume I

This hidden gem tucked away behind the awe-inspiring Basilica de Santa Maria del Mar is the workshop and showroom of two of Barcelona's most beautiful fashion brands. Name: womenswear is the creation of Irene Sabaté and Clara Aspachs and features casual linen trousers, flowing dresses and stylish sandals. The Lubochka brand complements Name:'s clothing with a timeless range of minimalist leather handbags and wallets designed by Russian artisan Olga Dubovik. Each piece is made in a small workshop in Barcelona using vegetable-tanned leather and other environmentally sustainable materials. Handbags start around 165€ and you can pick up an elegant wallet for around 115€, which is excellent value when you consider they're handcrafted in Barcelona.

LOCAL TIP
Stop at the nearby Museu de Cultures del Món (Carrer de Montcada, 12–14) to see a vast collection of ancient cultural relics from across the globe.

OSCAR H. GRAND

Carrer de la Barra de Ferro, 7
933 19 76 62
oscarhgrand.com
Open Tues–Sat 11.30am–
2.30pm & 4.30–8.30pm
Metro: Jaume I

In a neighbourhood where most boutiques are dedicated to womenswear, Oscar's contemporary tailoring for the modern gentleman offers an old-world shopping experience that even the most fashion-forward will revel in. Take your pick from hundreds of quality Italian and English fabrics, then let Oscar measure you up and craft bespoke items, from shirts and trousers to jackets and three-piece suits. There's also a ready-to-wear collection with more affordable shirts, trousers, jackets and belts. Oscar and his associates pride themselves on providing individualised customer service and are ready to help you dress to impress.

9.

CARRER DEL REC

Jutting off the main artery of Passeig del Born in two directions, Carrer del Rec is an ancient, porticoed street known for its independent boutiques and eateries. Under the arches at the lower end of the street, you'll find a number of tiny fashion boutiques such as **Almond**, **Visual Poetry**, and **La Comercial**, as well as cool cafes and cocktail bars like **La Hacienda**, where you can enjoy authentic Mexican dishes.

At the broader end of the street, you'll find more indie boutiques: check out **Dolores Promesas** for female fashion, **Le Swing** (*see* p. 053) for vintage finds and **Batallata** for modern menswear. The trendy bars and restaurants here are a hive of activity at all hours of the day. Squeeze into **Bormuth** for tapas, wine and people watching, and indulge in hearty burgers at **Pim Pam Burger**. Slip down Carrer del Sabateret and explore the many tapas stalls inside the **Mercat Princesa** food emporium housed in a 14th-century mansion.

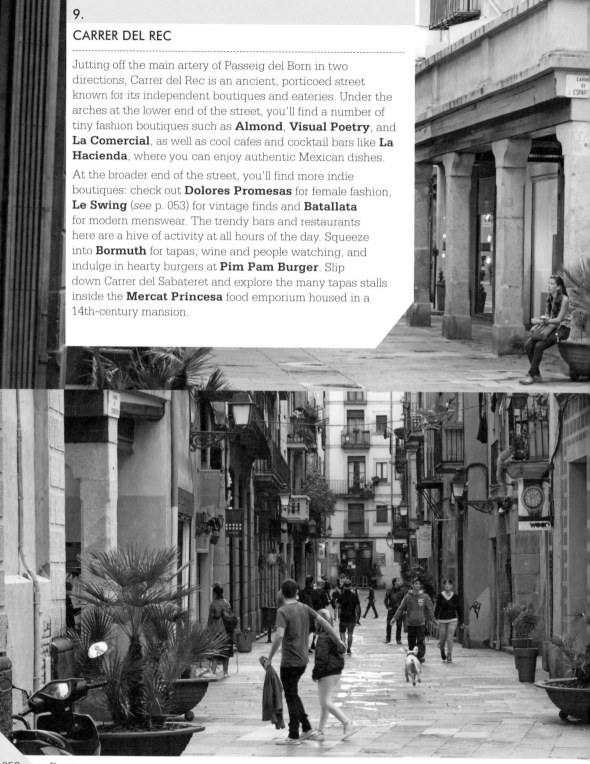

LOCAL TIP
Tucked away just off Carrer del Rec is the Arxiu Fotogràfic de Barcelona (Plaça de Pons i Clerch, 2, 2a. planta), a fascinating photographic archive that tells stories of Barcelona from 1839 to the present.

10.

BODEGA MAESTRAZGO

Carrer Sant Pere Més Baix, 90
933 10 26 73
facebook.com/
BodegaMaestrazgo
Open Mon–Thurs 11.30am–
3pm (lunch) & 4.30–10pm
(dinner), Fri–Sat 11am–10.30pm
Metro: Urquinaona

Those wanting to buy wine
in Spain traditionally would
pop into their local bodega
(wine shop) with an empty
bottle and buy by the litre –
they might even have sipped
a glass or two while waiting
for it to be filled. Most of
Barcelona's wine stores now
focus on selling bottled wine,
but Bodega Maestrazgo has
upheld bodega traditions
of old. Charmingly little has
changed at this family-run
warehouse-cum-wine bar
since it opened in 1952.
Manager José Moliner and
his crew weave through
boxes of wine, filling five-
litre bottles with local wine
from huge wooden barrels.
If you don't fancy lugging a
five-litre bottle around, grab
a seat at one of the rustic
wooden tables and ask for
a few recommendations.
Whether it's Catalan or
Galician, there's always an
exciting wine to try. Pop in
before lunch for an aperitivo
(pre-meal drink and snack) of
vermouth, olives and potato
chips for just 5€.

11.

BODEGA LA PUNTUAL

Carrer de Montcada, 22
933 10 35 45
bodegalapuntual.com
Open Mon–Sun 12pm–12am
Metro: Jaume I

Tucked inside a gorgeous
old building that dates
back to 1872, this bar and
restaurant is a tribute to the
joys of traditional Spanish
tapas. Legs of Iberian
jamón (ham) hang from the
ceiling and the shelves are
stacked with gourmet tins
of preserved shellfish – a
Catalonian delicacy.

The kitchen is open
from lunchtime straight
through to 12am (a rarity in
Barcelona) and is excellent
for everything from aperitivo
bites to hearty Spanish tapas.
Get your appetite going with
gourmet olives hand-stuffed
with anchovies, pickled
mussels and fresh oysters.
Other must-try tapas include
the tortilla de patatas, Spain's
signature potato omelette
that's lovingly made to order,
and the classic Catalan
trinxat de la Cerdanya, a fried
potato, cabbage and pork
patty adorned with a fried
egg. Ask if you can sit out in
the secret little courtyard to
enjoy your feast.

LOCAL TIP

One of Bodega La Puntual's owners, Joan Carles Ninou, owns legendary bodega (wine shop/bar) El Xampanyet next door. It's a little overrun with tourists, but worth elbowing in for a glass or two of the house-made cava.

11.

11.

10.

12

NAP

Avenida de Francesc Cambó, 30
686 19 26 90
facebook.com/nap.pizzeria
Open Mon–Fri 1.30–4.30pm
(lunch) & 8pm–12am (dinner),
Sat–Sun 1.30pm–12am
Metro: Jaume I

Spaniards tend to view
pizza as little more than a
rudimentary fast-food snack,
which means it can be tricky
to find a good slice, even
in a gourmet food hub like
Barcelona. That changed
for the better when NAP
(Neapolitan Authentic Pizza)
opened its doors in 2013.
The staff members and cooks
are Italian, and they turn out
wood-fired pizzas that are
worthy of Italian pride. Prices
here are very affordable; you
can indulge in a pizza and
a glass of Italian wine for
around 10€. The NAP pizzeria
in Born is the original (and
best) location; the second
location in Barceloneta
(Carrer Baluard, 69) is perfect
for a post-beach bite.

13.

BAR DEL PLA
Carrer de Montcada, 2
932 68 30 03
bardelpla.cat
Open Mon–Thurs 12–11pm,
Fri–Sat 12pm–12am
Metro: Jaume I

Located on what would have been medieval Barcelona's most glamorous street, Bar del Pla keeps the glamour alive with grand decor, first-class service and creative tapas at affordable prices. Try the thin-sliced raw mushrooms dressed with parmesan shavings, sliced strawberries and a mint-and-wasabi vinaigrette for a taste of their creative prowess. Some traditional flavours worth trying include Catalan cocas – a dish reminiscent of mini pizzas – topped with smoked sardines, mango and rocket (arugula). A four-strong team of sommeliers pours more than 100 Spanish wines (Bar del Pla's particularly well known for their organic and biodynamic offerings). It's worth booking a table ahead: the staff will happily muddle through the conversation in English if you're not a confident Spanish speaker.

14.

ELDISET
Carrer Antic de Sant Joan, 3
932 68 19 87
eldiset.com
Open Mon–Fri 7pm–3am,
Sat–Sun 1pm–3am
Metro: Jaume I

This is the place to go if you want to explore the many flavours of Catalan wine. While most bars and restaurants will carry a good selection of local wine varieties, Eldiset reserves almost all of its shelves and chillers for those from Catalonia. Explore robust reds from Priorat and Montsant, delicate whites and sparkling cavas from Penedès. The staff are trained sommeliers, so be sure to ask for recommendations on what to eat with your wine of choice. You can choose from a long list of traditional tapas, but Eldiset's forte is undoubtedly the torradas: crispy wedges of toasted bread topped with ingredients such as blue cheese and raspberry jam or black sausage with cured cheese and sundried tomatoes. Get there before 1pm on weekends to secure a table for lunch and before 8.30pm for dinner.

15

COLLAGE COCKTAIL BAR

Carrer dels Consellers, 4
931 79 37 85
Open Mon–Thurs 7pm–2.30am,
Fri–Sat 7pm–3am, Sun
7pm–2.30am
Metro: Jaume I

This hidden speakeasy-cum-art gallery is where Barcelona's mixologists go for after-work drinks. Local legend Fernando Requena and his team of alchemists shake up classic and creative cocktails behind its tiled bar, which glows fuchsia and green under antique lamps. The staff are more than happy to whip up and old-fashioned Negronis or Martinis, but they really come into their own when asked to create something on the spot. 'What do you normally like?' they ask. 'Bitter or sweet? Whisky? Rum? Vodka?' After flicking through a mental rolodex of options, they'll offer a few tailored suggestions. A personal favourite is the sweet-and-bitter Rum X X X, which goes down like honey. Ascend the stairs with your drink to the mezzanine level and sink into one of the antique sofas, surrounded by colourful paintings by local artists that cover the walls.

LOCAL TIP
Collage doesn't do food, but there's a great pizza place at the end of the street called Caputxes (Carrer Caputxes, 4) if you're in need of late-night fortification.

16

ANTIC TEATRE

Carrer de Verdaguer i Callís, 12
933 15 23 54
anticteatre.com
Open Thurs–Sun 4pm–12am
Metro: Urquinaona

There's a secret tucked away down narrow Carrer de Verdaguer i Callís: one that will make you feel as if you've stepped into another time and place. Behind Antic Teatre's concealed doorway is an ethereal garden bar and cultural space filled with fragrant flowerpots, huge trees that twinkle with the glow of fairy lights and yellow birdcages turned into ethereal lanterns. As well as being an excellent place to sneak off to for a drink, it has an indoor stage that's a great place to enjoy works by local artists. Regular exhibitions and performances range from live music shows and poetry readings to comedy acts and independent film screenings. Check out the website for the latest program, or turn up and enjoy whatever happens to be on that day.

PALAU DALMASES

Carrer de Montcada, 20
933 10 06 73
palaudalmases.com
Open Mon–Sun 11.30–1.30am
Metro: Jaume I

This candlelit 17th-century Baroque palace bursts to life every night with the entrancing sights and sounds of traditional flamenco. Built for the Catalan aristocrat Pau Ignasi de Dalmases i Ros, its internal courtyard and spiral staircase adorned with sculptures of mythological beings alone is worth a visit. Dancers perform to live flamenco guitar and percussive cajón (a box-shaped instrument) in the intimate performance area under a series of vaulted ceilings, surrounded by ancient oil paintings hanging from the stone walls. The whole experience feels like enjoying art in a noble's home with a glass of good Spanish sangria in hand. Thursday nights are reserved for the Petita Companyia Lírica de Barcelona, which gives great opera performances. There are three shows per night (at 6, 7.30 and 9.30pm). Try to make it to the 7.30pm show when the performers are warmed up, but not fatigued.

16.

17.

17.

16.

16.

17.

Parc de la Ciutadella (Passeig de Picasso, 21) is Barcelona's leafiest public park, perfect for an afternoon picnic or siesta. It harbours the imposing **Arc de Triomf** and **Castell dels Tres Dragons**, built for the 1888 Universal Exhibition, Barcelona's zoo, a picturesque rowing-boat lake and the regal **Cascada fountain and waterfall**, which is one of the city's premiere photography spots. Legend has it that Antoni Gaudí, Barcelona's beloved architect, contributed to the design when he was a young apprentice.

Don't miss the **Merado del Santa Caterina food market** (Avinguda de Francesc Cambó, 16) and its sinuous, multi-coloured roof designed to reflect the freshness of the produce inside. It is every bit as beautiful as the more famous Mercat de la Boqueria on La Rambla (see p. 039), but with fewer tourists.

Get your culture fix at the **Museu Picasso** (Carrer Montcada, 15–23, museupicasso.bcn. cat/en, free entry on the first Sunday of every month) and the neighbouring **Museu de Culturer del Mon** (Carrer de Montcada, 12–14, museuculturesmon.bcn.cat/en), both housed in old, noble palaces.

Fintan Kerr is owner and head sommelier at Wine Cuentista wine tastings (Carrer de Sant Pere Més Baix, 92 winecuenista. com), which hosts wine tastings led by qualified sommeliers meant to help people discover the treasure trove of Spanish wine.

Basilica Santa Maria del Mar (Plaça de Santa Maria, 1): Dating back to 1372, this is one of the most beautiful churches in Barcelona and a place I often head towards to take a little peaceful time for myself.

El Born Centre de Cultura i Memòna (Plaça Comercial, 12): These ancient city ruins date back to the 1700s and provide fascinating insights into Barcelona's roots.

Devour Barcelona Tours (devourbarcelonafoodtours.com): The 'Tapas Taverns and History' tour is a really fun way to explore this ancient neighbourhood's fascinating history and eat at all the best bars.

Passeig del Born: Take a stroll down Born's main artery and take a moment to envision the jousting tournaments that used to take place here.

CIUTADELLA
VILA OLÍMPICA

Parc del
Port Olímpic

LA VILA
OLÍMPICA DEL
POBLENOU

Plaça
dels
Voluntaris

Parc de
Carles I

Hotel Arts

Port
Olímpic

Parc
de les
Cascades

OPIUM

Somorrostro

Platja

Parc de la
Barceloneta

TO
MAP RIGHT
(VIA PASSEIG MARÍTIM
DE LA BARCELONETA)

Platja de la Barceloneta

BARCELONETA

Lining the city's shoreline and the glitzy Port Vell Marina, Barceloneta is a maze of salty streets that revolves around the sea. The city's historic fishermen's quarter has working-class roots that can still be felt in its ancient markets and seafood tapas bars, contrasted spectacularly by its lively, nightclub-riddled beachfront.

You could easily find yourself eating traditional paella at a 100-year-old hole-in-the-wall one minute, then sipping cocktails on a rooftop terrace the next. It's wild and decadent, traditional and conservative – in other words, quintessential Barcelona.

24

SHOP, EAT AND DRINK
1 MAREMÀGNUM

EAT
2 BALUARD BAKERY

EAT AND DRINK
3 LA COVA FUMADA
4 CAL PAPI
5 BLACKLAB BREWHOUSE &
   KITCHEN

17

6 CAN SOLÉ
7 BACOA
8 SALT BEACH CLUB
9 ECLIPSE SKYBAR
10 ABSENTA BAR

DRINK
11 OPIUM

BARCELONETA

H10 Port Vell Hotel

MUSEU D'HISTÒRIA DE CATALUNYA

CARRER DE GINEBRA

CAN MAÑO

TO OPIUM (SEE MAP LEFT)

L4

La Cara de Barcelona

BLACKLAB BREWHOUSE & KITCHEN

CARRER DE LA MAQUINISTA

MERCAT DE LA BARCELONETA

CARRER D'ANDREA DORIA

EL GÒTIC

MOLL DEL DIPÒSIT

LA BOMBETA

BALUARD BAKERY

L'ÒSTIA

ESGLÉSIA DE SANT MIQUEL DEL PORT

ABSENTA BAR

Dàrsena del Comerç

LA COVA FUMADA

CAL PAPI

Platja de la Barceloneta

CAN SOLÉ

CARRER DE SANT CARLES

Dàrsena National

CIUTAT VELLA

CARRER DE L'ALMIRALL CERVERA

MOLOKA'I SUP CENTER

L'Aquàrium Barcelona

Port Vell

NAP

CARRER DE L'ALMIRALL AIXADA

CAN MAJÓ

Cines Maremàgnum

MOLL DEL RELLOTGE

BACOA

LA BARCELONETA

Platja de Sant Miquel

MAREMÀGNUM

PASSEIG DE JOAN DE BORBÓ

Miraestels

INTERNACIONAL MAREMÀGNUM

Dàrsena de la Indústria

TORRE DE SANT SEBASTIÀ

Aeri del Port de Barcelona

MAR MEDITERRÀNIA

INTERNACIONAL NORD

World Trade Center

Moll de Barcelona

PASSEIG DE JOAN DE BORBÓ

PASSEIG MARE NOSTRUM

Sant Sebastià

Platja

N

MOLL DE CATALUNYA

SALT BEACH CLUB

0   100 m

MOLL OCCIDENTAL

PASSEIG DE JOAN DE BORBÓ

W Hotel

PLAÇA DE LA ROSA DELS VENTS

ECLIPSE SKYBAR

1.

MAREMÀGNUM

Moll d'Espanya, 5
932 25 81 00
es.club-onlyou.com/Maremagnum
Open Mon–Sun 10am–10pm
Metro: Drassanes

Built on a quasi-floating island in the middle of Port Vell, this shimmering mega-mall boasts more than 35 designer fashion stores in one location. Conveniently located across a beautiful footbridge near the bottom of the busy boulevard of La Rambla, there's always a buzz in the air and something for everyone, including the Barcelona Aquarium. The FC Botiga is an official store of the Barcelona football team, which means it stocks one of the city's most comprehensive selections for soccer fans. Chain restaurants sprawl over the terraces, while more exclusive restaurants on the upper levels offer impressive views out over the marina. This isn't a culinary destination to write home about, but trendy Café del Mar is worth a quick cocktail pit stop, especially to see the sun set over the city and the Mediterranean waters.

2

BALUARD BAKERY
Carrer del Baluard, 38
932 21 12 08
baluardbarceloneta.com
Open Mon–Sat 8am–9pm
Metro: Barceloneta

The Spanish aren't known for their breadmaking skills: ask for a basket of bread and you'll likely be served something liable to chip a tooth. Enter fourth-generation baker Anna Bellsolà, who is changing Barcelona's bread scene with her hearty artisanal loaves. As roaring ovens fill this flour-dusted space with joyful aromas, locals line up for everything from crispy baguettes and rustic pa de pagès (country bread) to dense rye and elaborate sourdough stuffed full of gourmet olives, herbs and dried fruit. Every batch is made using only the highest quality organic stone-milled flour and is baked in wood-fired stone ovens. Grab a bag of croissants, brioche cakes and pastries and stroll over to the beach for a simple, satisfying breakfast. There's a second Baluard Bakery tucked inside the Praktik Hotel (Carrer de Provença, 279) in Dreta de l'Eixample (see p. 109) where the almond croissants are to die for.

3.

LA COVA FUMADA

Carrer del Baluard, 56
932 21 40 61
facebook.com/pages/La-Cova-Fumada/167510036619950
Open Mon–Wed 9am–3.15pm,
Thurs–Fri 9am–3.15pm (lunch)
& 6–8.10pm (dinner), Sat
9am–1pm
Metro: Barceloneta

There's no sign outside
this nondescript hotspot for
traditional tapas and fresh
seafood, which means it flies
way under most tourists'
radars – this place is as
authentic as it gets. Located
in lively Plaça del Poeta
Boscà, it opened in the 1940s
to cater to local fishermen
and dockworkers and is
still run by the same family
today. There's no menu,
but the ever-magnanimous
Josep María and Magí Sole,
grandsons of founder Maria
Pla, are happy to reel off a list
of recommendations based
on what came in fresh that
morning. Expect dishes like
crispy fried sardines and
grilled calamari with garlic,
chopped parsley and lemon
juice. The must-try dish is the
bomba, the meat-and-potato
croquette that Maria Pla
invented during the Civil War
to resemble the little hand
grenades that local anarchists
used. They're best ordered
spicy. La Cava Fumada
doesn't take reservations, but
if you order a beer and hang
around long enough, they'll
squeeze you in.

4.

CAL PAPI

Carrer de l'Atlàntida, 65
932 21 85 64
calpapi.es
Open Tues–Sat 12–10.30pm,
Sun 12–4.30pm
Metro: Barceloneta

Tucked away on a quiet
backstreet just steps from
Barceloneta beach, this
traditional, marine-themed
tapas restaurant cooks up
some of the city's freshest
seafood. As you duck through
the warped wooden doors,
you can't help but feel as if
you're climbing down into
the bowels of a ship. Fishing
nets and old ropes hang
from wood-panelled ceilings,
framing animated groups of
locals huddled around wine
barrels, sharing seasonal
tapas and the bargain house
wine. Expect doughnut-sized
calamari, steaming bowls of
fresh mussels, and scallops
served with wedges of lemon.
This is an excellent place
to try fideuà, a traditional
noodle version of paella. Chef
Carmen personally delivers it
from the kitchen with a proud
grin and a few friendly words.

5.

BLACKLAB BREWHOUSE & KITCHEN

Plaça de Pau Vila, 1
932 21 83 60
blacklab.es
Open Sun–Thurs 12pm–
1.30am, Fri–Sat 12pm–2am
Metro: Barceloneta

This warehouse-like space created by Chinese-American couple Jing Chen and Matt Boder was Barcelona's first brewpub and is still one of its best. Taste your way through some of the 30 house-brewed craft beers, which include the Claudia IPA with hints of citrus and aromas of mango and papaya. Their small-batch seasonal brews are a little more experimental, with beers like the Japanese Tea IPA with subtle hints of jasmine and orange peel. If you're feeling adventurous, try one of the brewmasters' beer cocktails. The Dark & Stormy (rum, lime juice and ginger syrup with BlackLab Sunday Pils) is a winner on a hot day. The meaty menu offers classic American beer-chugging dishes like spicy buffalo wings with blue cheese and the 200-gram (7 oz) BlackLab Burger, as well as Asian-inspired offerings like slow-roasted chicken marinated with house spices, vanilla, jalapeños and homemade hoisin sauce.

LOCAL TIP
Be sure to pop into the lively Mercat de la Barceloneta (Plaça Poeta Bosca, 1), an airy food market located just a short stroll away.

6.

CAN SOLÉ

Carrer de Sant Carles, 4
932 21 50 12
restaurantcansole.com
Open Tues–Thurs 1–4pm
(lunch) & 8–11pm (dinner),
Fri–Sat 1–4pm (lunch) &
8.30–11pm (dinner)
Metro: Barceloneta

Opened in 1903, this seafood restaurant has a colourful facade and original decor that provide a glimpse into old-world Barceloneta. The refined dining room has hardly changed in more than 100 years: its elegant round tables draped in crisp white tablecloths are perfect for those important occasions when you don't mind splashing out a little extra for authentic cuisine. The walls are covered with photos of local celebrities who have dined here, including iconic Catalan artists Joan Miró and Antoni Tàpies. Owner José María has been in charge since 1975 and, though similar establishments have let their standards slip as tourist numbers increase, he continues to serve top-quality dishes. Start with sepias troceadas (slow-baked squid in a rich tomato salsa), followed by a sizzling pan of Can Solé paella and some of the hearty, abuela (grandma)-style cakes. The best place to eat is on the ground floor next to the open kitchen, where you can watch chef Mari Carme do her thing.

LOCAL TIP
The Spanish wouldn't dream of eating paella for dinner (they believe it's too heavy), so you'll find the best paellas served at lunchtime.

7

BACOA

Carrer Judici, 15
932 77 61 75
bacoaburger.com
Open Mon–Thurs 12pm–1am,
Fri–Sun 12pm–2am
Metro: Barceloneta

Barcelona has long been obsessed with the joys of the humble burger, but it wasn't until Australian chef Brad Ainsworth and his Spanish wife, Paula Lera, opened Bacoa that the phrase 'gourmet burger' entered the local vernacular. With the laid-back vibes of a traditional Australian barbecue and a Mediterranean respect for quality ingredients, these beautiful burgers are some of the city's best. The beef is organic and sourced from a small farm in the Catalan Pyrenees. The pickles and sauces, from the tomato sauce and mustard to the black truffle mayo and aioli, are all made on-site. Order the Australiana burger topped with grilled beetroot, cheddar, bacon and barbecue sauce and a side of rustic fries. For something less hefty, try the Pollo Light, which is marinated chicken breast with mustard and roasted red peppers wedged into a wholemeal bun.

8.

SALT BEACH CLUB

Passeig del Mare Nostrum, 19–21
932 95 28 19
saltbeachclub.com
Open (April) Sun–Thurs 1–5pm, Fri–Sat 1pm–12am; (May–Sept) Mon–Sun 1pm–1am
Metro: Barceloneta

You know summer has arrived in Barcelona when the chiringuitos (temporary beach bars) suddenly appear on the sand. They are all charming, with their 'deserted tropical island' vibes, but Salt Beach Club has really perfected the concept. Sink into one of the designer lounges in the shade of a palm tree and sip piña coladas with your toes in the sand and a sea breeze in your hair. This sophisticated beach club is run by the five-star W Hotel, located within spitting distance of the water's edge. The model-esque staff provide excellent service and a range of cocktails. Whilst the old-school chiringuitos down the coast serve up microwaved marvels, here at Salt you can enjoy fresh crab salads and gourmet smokehouse burgers at reasonable prices. Go between 5 and 9pm on Friday, Saturday and Sunday nights for the 'Summer Sounds' DJ sets.

9.

ECLIPSE SKYBAR

W Hotel, Plaça de la Rosa dels
Vents, 1
93 295 28 00
eclipse-barcelona.com
Open Mon–Thurs 6pm–3am,
Fri–Sun 6pm–4am
Metro: Barceloneta

Occupying the 26th floor of
the luxury W Hotel, Eclipse
SkyBar is the place to party if
you want panoramic views,
creative cocktails and some
of Europe's coolest DJs.
Designed by local interior
designer Isabel López Vilalta,
the futuristic furniture and
sinuous ceiling lights fill
the space with a neon-
pink-and-blue glow. It feels
more like a spaceship than
a hotel bar, but the swells
of glamorous people are
constant reminders that
you are in one of the world's
most exciting cities. Sip on
Catalan cava before moving
on to a signature Watermelon
Martini. The sushi is good,
and surprisingly well priced.
Order the Moriawase
assortment, which includes
20 pieces of sashimi and
nigiri for 36€. Arrive at
Eclipse SkyBar before 10pm
to secure one of the coveted
window seats.

10.
ABSENTA BAR

Carrer de Sant Carles, 36
932 21 36 38
absenta.bar
Open Sun–Thurs 11–2am,
Fri–Sat 11–3am
Metro: Barceloneta

This secluded bar is one of the city's original absinthe watering holes and one of its most atmospheric. In the late 1800s, Barcelona's aristocrats and bohemians grew increasingly enamoured of the mind-expanding qualities of absinthe, and Absenta still offers 20 homemade types. The quirky space is filled with rickety antique furniture, old gas lamps and wooden cabinets filled with glowing red and green absinthe medicine bottles. Harlequin puppets and Mexican Day of the Dead skeletons hang from the rafters, while a huge green-winged fairy leers serenely from over the bar. Pair your absinthe with something from the excellent tapas menu – the Argentinian empanadas (meat-stuffed pastries) are superb. But go easy: this is, after all, what Vincent Van Gogh was drinking when he decided to chop his ear off.

11.
OPIUM

Passeig Marítim, 34
932 25 91 00
opiumbarcelona.com
Open Mon–Sun 12pm–6am
Metro: Barceloneta

With its exclusive terrace just off the beach and DJ sets from global megastars like David Guetta, Tiesto, and Avicii, Opium is one of the most happening clubs in Barcelona. During the day, it's all about posing with an expensive cocktail and people watching on the club's white sofas. There's also a restaurant, but this is no place for eating – this is a place to see and be seen. The beats start picking up at sunset, attracting the rich and beautiful, and grind on until sunrise. Prices reflect the kind of clientele the club wants to attract (expect to pay 20€ to get in and around 10€ for even the most basic drinks), but you can't put a price on this kind of glamour. Dress to impress, or you may not get past the doorman. Visit the You Barcelona website (youbarcelona.com) to get on Opium's guest list and enjoy free entry before 2am.

Check out the La Maquinista Terrestre y Marítima (Carrer de la Maquinista). This huge factory dating back to 1855 once employed more than 1000 workers and produced no less than 569 locomotive steam trains.

11.

10.

11.

Passeig de Joan de Borbó is Barceloneta's main thoroughfare; it has been ravished by tourism, but plenty of old gems continue to thrive. Take a stroll and stop off to watch the live bands that spring up to give spontaneous performances in the sun.

Dart down little side streets to find scenes of local daily life. **Plaça de la Barceloneta** harbours the gorgeous **Sant Miquel del Port** parish church, which was completed in 1755. The lively **Plaça del Poeta Boscà** is the neighbourhood's nucleus, a lively square where families play football and ping-pong, and generally hang out and catch up on the latest gossip. The thriving market **Mercat de la Barceloneta** (mercatsbcn.cat) is located here and is well worth perusing.

Rent a bike from one of the many rental shops along Passeig de Joan de Borbó and cruise down **Passeig Marítim** towards the avant-garde W Hotel. Behind the property you'll find the huge terraced **Plaça de la Rosa dels Vents**, where crowds gather to enjoy expansive views across the beach and the cobalt Mediterranean Sea.

Cool off in the translucent water or rent a paddleboard from the **Moloka'i SUP Center** (Carrer de Meer, 39, molokaisupcenter.com). In the winter months when there are waves, you can also enjoy surfing and windsurfing.

David Baird is founder and captain at Classic Sail Barcelona (classicsailbcn. com.) and offers private sailing trips on *Gemini*, his antique sailboat.

La Bombeta (Calle de la Maquinista, 3): This busy, informal, excellent tapas bar is the home of the original bomba (or so they say – it's a bit of a hotly contested topic), a ball of mashed potato with a meat filling and a spicy sauce. Come here in a group and order up a bunch of plates to share. Cheap bottles of cold, tart turbio wine still cloudy with yeast are perfect to wash down the heaps of fried and grilled food.

Can Maño (Carrer del Baluard, 12): This place is a local legend, offering fish that's come straight off the boat. There's nothing fancy here: tiny tables squeezed into a couple of small rooms, the menu hand-written on the wall with today's catch and very fresh, simple food. A fisherman's restaurant with fisherman's prices. They don't take reservations, so turn up early.

Forn de Pa Baluard (Baluard Bakery) (Carrer del Baluard, 38): People come from all across the city to buy their bread and pastries from this excellent bakery. The pastries are to die for, but this is where I get my fix of good old-fashioned crusty bread. It's heaven!

Museu de d'Historia de Catalunya (Moll de la Barceloneta): (Palau de Mar, Plaça de Pau Vila, 3) This fascinating museum provides an excellent and accessible explanation of Catalonia's origins. Displays range from the Stone Age through the Civil War era. End your visit with a drink on the rooftop terrace and enjoy the excellent views across the port.

LA FARMERA

TORRE GLÒRIES (TORRE AGBAR)

PLAÇA DE LES GLÒRIES CATALANES

MUSEU DEL DISSENY DE BARCELONA

CNMC BUILDING

T5 T6

GLÒRIES

ENCANTS VELLS MARKET

EL PARC I LA LLACUNA DEL POBLENOU

CARRER DE TÀNGER

CARRER DE SANCHO D'AVILA

CARRER DE BADAJOZ

TO MAP RIGHT →

AVINGUDA MERIDIANA

Museu de la Música

T4

RAZZMATAZZ

CARRER DE D'ÀLABA

AUDITORI/ TEATRE NACIONAL

R2 Sud R13 R14 R15 R16

Capri By Fraser Barcelona

CARRER DELS ALMOGAVERS

CARRER DE PALLARS

RG1 R1 R3 R4 R12

L1

MARINA

MARINA

BOGATELL

CARRER DE

L4

POBLENOU

Coastal Poblenou ('New Village' in Catalan) grew up around the booming 19th-century textiles industry that led to its nickname, 'The Manchester of Catalonia'. The industry eventually declined, and the area fell into disrepair. Then along came the 1992 Olympic Games, kickstarting the neighbourhood's transformation from dusty industrial centre to hipster hub.

These days, Poblenou is more Brooklyn than Manchester, with a wealth of world-class street art and strong contrasts between old and new. Luxury hotels and apartments line the shore, distinguished by the colour-changing, 38-storey Torre Glòries (Torre Agbar). It's relaxed for an inner-city neighbourhood and many tourists don't explore it, making it ideal for tuning into the local pace of life.

24   JUN 8076

SHOP
1 FESTUK

SHOP, EAT AND DRINK
2 PALO ALTO MARKET
3 ENCANTS VELLS MARKET

EAT
4 EL TÍO CHÉ

17

EAT AND DRINK
5 EL 58
6 ELS PESCADORS
7 LA CERVECITA NUESTRA DE CADA DÍA

DRINK
8 MADAME GEORGE
9 GARAGE BEER Co. BREWERY
10 NIU ESPAI ARTÍSTIC
11 RAZZMATAZZ

↑ TO
GARAGE BEER CO. BREWERY
(NOT SHOWN ON MAP)

0   200 m

SELYA
DE MAR

PROVENÇALS
DEL POBLENOU

MUHBA
Oliva
Artés

CARRER DE
BAC DE RODA

AVINGUDA DIAGONAL

SELYA
DE MAR

Parc
del Centre
del Poblenou

FLUYIÀ

DIAGONAL
MAR I EL FRONT
MARÍTIM DEL
POBLENOU

CARRER DE BILBAO

AVINGUDA DIAGONAL

SANT
MARTÍ

N

CARRER DE BAC DE RODA

PALO ALTO
MARKET

T4

Meliá
Barcelona
Sky Hotel

Jardins
Teresa
de Calcuta

CARRER DE PERE IV

PERE IV

CARRER DE PERE IV

CARRER DE BILBAO

CARRER DE PALLARS

L4

Jardins de
Josep
Trueta

Jardins
de Gandhi

CARRER DE LLULL

CARRER D'ESPRONCEDA

Jardins de
Remedios
Varo

CARRER DE

RAMBLA DEL

POBLENOU

CARRER DE

POBLENOU

Jardins de
Simone
de Beauvoir

PASSEIG DEL TAULAT

Jardins de
Joan Fuster
i Ortells

NIU
ESPAI
ARTÍSTIC

CARRER DE LA LLACUNA

MADAME
GEORGE

MINYAM

MARIA

Plaça de
Julio
González

Jardins de
Jaime Gil
de Biedma

PASSEIG DE GARCIA FÀRIA

Holiday Inn
Express

FESTUK

AGUILÓ

CARRER DE BILBAO

Eurohotel
Diagonal
Port

CARRER DE PALLARS

EL 58

EL TÍO CHÉ

RONDA LITORAL

LA CERVECITA
NUESTRA DE
CADA DIA

RAMBLA

DEL

CARRER DEL TAULAT

ELS
PESCADORS

LLACUNA

TO
RAZZMATAZZ
(SEE MAP LEFT)

CARRER

DE

LLULL

EL
POBLENOU

POBLENOU

Parc
del
Poblenou

DEL LITORAL

CARRER DE RAMON TURRÓ

CARRER DEL TAULAT

BASE
NÀUTICA

CARRER DE BADAJOZ

Cementiri
de l'Est
(Poblenou)

Hotel 4
Barcelona

CARRER, CARMEN AMAYA

Parc
del
Poblenou

Bed and
Beach
Barcelona

AVINGUDA D'ICÀRIA

RONDA LITORAL

AVINGUDA DEL BOGATELL

Platja del Bogatell

MAR
MEDITERRÀNIA

LA VILA
OLÍMPICA
DEL
POBLENOU

SB Icaria
Barcelona

TO
ENCANTS
VELLS MARKET
(SEE MAP LEFT)

1.

FESTUK

Rambla del Poblenou, 67
932 21 82 09
festuk.com
Open Mon–Sat 10.30am–2pm
& 5–8.30pm
Metro: Llacuna

Festuk caters to local urbanites with a youthful range of cool, comfortable fashion. This green-lit space is filled with stock largely aimed at female shoppers, but there's plenty on offer to keep male companions occupied. Peruse the rails for organic cotton dresses from Basque label SkunkFunk and elegant bomber jackets from Scandinavian brand Desires. The shoe racks are filled with everything from beach-friendly slip-ons made by Maians using natural and minimalist fabrics to Fly London boots and sandals. They have regular clearout sales, where prices are slashed by up to 50 per cent. Have a look at the Outlet section on their website for a glimpse at the treasure you might find instore.

LOCAL TIP
Stop in at the Niu contemporary arts space (Carrer dels Almogàvers, 208), where you can connect with local creatives and explore avant-garde music, photography and art.

2

PALO ALTO MARKET
Carrer dels Pellaires, 30
931 59 66 70
paloaltomarket.com/en/home
Open 11am–9pm (1st Sat & Sun
of the month, except August)
Metro: Selva de Mar

Held in the verdant gardens of one of Poblenou's many abandoned factories, Palo Alto is Barcelona's hippest street market. This hotbed of creativity showcases some of the city's best independent fashion designers, musicians and artists. Browse its little lanes and hidden nooks, where you'll find handcrafted clothing, homewares, accessories and jewellery from local designers. The creators are always excited to talk about their products, which adds an extra level of intimacy to the experience.

The main Street Market harbours a selection of food trucks where you can indulge in everything from gourmet burgers and tacos to traditional Spanish paella and pulpo (octopus). Those with a sweet tooth will find artisanal ice-cream, cakes and coffee.

Palo Alto is sponsored by Moritz beer, Aperol and Torres wine, which means there are plenty of bars at which to grab a drink while you hunt for treasures. Entry tickets are cheaper when you buy them from their website, so try to book ahead.

3.

ENCANTS VELLS MARKET
Carrer de los Castillejos, 158
932 46 30 30
encantsbcn.com
Open Mon, Wed & Fri–Sat
9am–8pm
Metro: Glòries

Founded in 1300, this gargantuan flea market is one of the oldest of its kind in Europe. It covers three levels and a total of 15,000 square metres (161,459 square feet), a warren of narrow alleys lined with hundreds of stalls that sell a myriad of *encants vells* (old charms). Browse for vintage cameras, furniture, paintings, clothing and jewellery. There's new stock too: stallholders hawk everything from paella pans to 'designer' underwear and watches. If you aren't afraid to haggle, you'll be sure to find a few *gangas* (bargains). Get there before 10am if you're interested in antiques as the real treasures get snapped up by the early birds.

A small food court hidden away on the top floor – try the excellent pescaditos (little fried fish) at Peixet – offers elevated views over the iconic Torre Glòries (Torre Agbar) next door. But the main draw is the market's futuristic design, completed in 2013. It bounces light around the cavernous space in a way that makes it look more like a *Star Wars* spaceship than a market.

LOCAL TIP

The iconic, 38-storey Torre Glòries (Torre Agbar) is one of the city's tallest buildings. The facade is clad with nearly 60,000 panels of painted aluminium and glass that change colour depending on how the light hits them.

4.

EL TÍO CHÉ

Rambla del Poblenou, 44–46
933 09 18 72
eltioche.es
Open Sun–Thurs 10–1am,
Fri–Sat 10–2am
Metro: Llacuna

You'll stumble across untouched relics of the past tucked between Poblenou's futuristic office blocks and hipster cocktail bars. El Tío Ché is one of these: a 100-year-old horchateria (horchata bar) famous for its artisanal ice-cream and pastries, with an open-fronted facade that boasts its original flamboyant mosaic tiles and vintage signage. You'll no longer find Tío Ché ('Uncle Ché') behind the counter, but fifth-generation family members always make a fuss over their customers. Horchata is a sort of Spanish take on the milkshake, but made with naturally sweet tigernuts. The classic way to drink it is with a bag of freshly baked fartons (long pastry fingers sprinkled with powdered sugar) that are perfect for dunking. Enjoy your horchata with a giant scoop of homemade ice-cream and a slab of sticky turrón (nougat). El Tío Ché was also the first importer of German sausages in Barcelona, so make sure to try a hotdog.

5.

EL 58

Rambla del Poblenou, 58
932 95 28 19
facebook.com/el58poblenou
Open Tues–Sat 1.30–11pm,
Sun 1–4pm
Metro: Llacuna

With its bare-brick walls, comic book-lined cupboards and creative tapas, El 58 epitomises the casual-cool vibes that define this once-industrial neighbourhood. Whether you're in the mood for a quick glass of wine and a few nibbles or an informal lunch, this relaxed cafe-cum-restaurant has something to suit. Its owners, Frenchman Jerome Misan and Catalonian Amos Martínez, elevate traditional tapas and raciones (rations) with international ingredients to create interesting fusion flavours you won't find elsewhere. Try sharing plates of homemade hummus and seasonal salads, Andalusian-style eggplant with honey and Asian-influenced dishes like salmon tataki and marinated chicken with wasabi mayonnaise. The antique tables and wooden chairs give it the feel of a Parisian cafe, while the internal patio, complete with bistro furniture and dainty plant plots, is Poblenou all the way. They don't take bookings, so be sure to arrive a little before 1pm to ensure you're first in the door.

6.

ELS PESCADORS

Plaça de Prim, 1
932 25 20 18
elspescadors.com
Open Mon–Sun 1–4pm (lunch)
& 8–11pm (dinner)
Metro: Llacuna

Set in idyllic Plaça Prim in an old tavern dating back to 1848, Els Pescadors ('The Fishermen') is one of the city's oldest and most respected seafood restaurants. You'll find all sorts of great dishes here, but it's the rice and seafood that keep the locals coming back. Start with sea anemone fritters and steamed mussels with onion, apple and ginger. Then try the house special bomba fishermen's rice, laced with chunks of three different types of fish, depending on what came in fresh that morning. The dining room by the bar is the original tavern space, featuring the same marble tables and rickety wooden chairs that used to prop up local fishermen and factory workers. The outside terrace is where you want to be on a sunny day, with views over the tucked-away square's unusual, sprawling ombús trees. The staff is cheery in a 'whistle while we work' kind of way, and the area retains the atmosphere of the lazy seaside village it used to be.

7.

LA CERVECITA NUESTRA DE CADA DIA

Carrer de Llull, 184
934 86 92 71
facebook.com/
Lacervecitanuestradecadadia
Open Mon–Thurs 6–10pm,
Fri–Sat 11.30am–2pm (lunch)
& 6–11pm (dinner), Sun 6–10pm
Metro: Llacuna

This tranquil bottle shop and bar, whose name translates to 'Our Daily Little Beer', boasts more than 200 craft beers from all over the globe. Its lofty space, stacked to the rafters with boxes and kegs, makes it easy to imagine this old industrial unit's former life as a workshop. The vibe is relaxed and informal, cultivated by husband-and-wife duo Kim and Angie who are passionate about sharing their love for good brewing. Ask for recommendations and prepare to taste anything from classic Belgian Tripels to Catalan IPAs and sour American wild ales. Don't miss their homemade brews, which include the hop-tastic Júlia IPA, named after the couple's daughter. If you're keen to try a few different local beers and have a chat with the staff, then stop by on your way to dinner, before it gets too rowdy. The tasty selection of tapas make ideal appetisers.

8

MADAME GEORGE

Carrer de Pujades, 179
935 00 51 51
madamegeorgebar.com
Open Mon–Thurs 6pm–2am,
Fri–Sat 6pm–3am,
Sun 6pm–12.30am
Metro: Llacuna

Entering this theatrical cocktail bar is like stepping through a wormhole back to the 1920s. Its owners, Peruvian Melina Ramirez and Irishman Daragh O'Donnell, worked with local interior designer Daniel Spinella to combine a mélange of gilded antique mirrors, silken wingback armchairs and plush fabric wallpapers, complete with romantic touches like opulent chandeliers and candelabras. You'll half expect Mr Gatsby himself to step out from behind the turquoise curtains. The bar's well-stocked shelf hints at a diverse range of cocktails. House specials include The Pepigroso (vodka or gin, cucumber, mint, lime and ginger beer) and Melina's speciality Peruvian Pisco Sour. On Friday nights, the Art Deco vibe is paired with DJs spinning funk, soul and disco. Keep an eye on the website to hear about their latest drag shows.

LOCAL TIP

Madame George doesn't do food, but trendy Minyam next door (Carrer de Pujades, 187) is a real treat for creative tapas. Don't miss the ceviche!

9.

GARAGE BEER CO. BREWERY

Carrer de Sant Adrià, 66
933 60 79 40
facebook.com/pages/Garage-Beer-Co/142998666222113
Open Mon–Thurs 5pm–12am,
Fri–Sat 5pm–3am,
Sun 5pm–12am
Metro: Sant Andreu

Garage Beer Co. exploded onto Barcelona's craft beer scene in 2015 when they opened a brewpub in Eixample (Carrer del Consell de Cent, 261). It wasn't long before owners Alberto Zamborlin and James Welsh were looking to expand: the duo crowdfunded more than 500,000€ (in just three weeks) to create their dream brewery, which takes up over 1000 square metres (10,764 square feet) and has the capacity to brew 3500 litres (925 gallons) at a time. The best part is the 'creative area', where brewers try out ideas and launch their latest creations. Try staples like the quaffable Riba lager and rotating releases like the Soup IPA and the Romaní pilsner made with honey from romani bees raised on local rosemary bushes.

Live music, DJs and plenty of shop talk is par for the course at their tasting parties. Find out about upcoming parties on their Facebook page and be sure to register your attendance.

LOCAL TIP
Check out Parc del Fòrum (Muelle de la Marina Seca, Carrer de la Pau, 12) on the waterfront. This expansive concrete event space was built to host the 2004 Universal Forum of Cultures and now hosts Barcelona's hottest music festivals.

10.

NIU ESPAI ARTÍSTIC

Carrer dels Almogàvers, 208
933 56 88 11
niubcn.com
Open Tues–Sat 5–10pm
Metro: Llacuna

Much like the rest of Poblenou, Niu Espai Artístic (New Arts Space) is constantly looking to the future, with progressive audiovisual and multimedia art exhibitions as well as live music and dance performances. You never know what you might discover: the sounds of experimental electronica and 'laptop orchestras' will feature one day, while the next might offer surrealist theatre and mind-expanding 4D cinematography. There are more traditional exhibits too, with pieces from emerging painters and street artists. Hands-on workshops offer visitors the opportunity to try something new, like becoming a visual projection artist or making a mean beat with a sample machine. The bar is well stocked with local beers and wines to help expand your mind while you enjoy the exhibits.

11

RAZZMATAZZ

Carrer dels Almogàvers, 122
933 20 82 00
salarazzmatazz.com
Open Wed–Sat 12–6am
Metro: Marina

A night at Razzmatazz feels like being at an indoor music festival. Barcelona's biggest, wildest nightclub is housed in a colossal warehouse containing five distinct spaces, each pumping out an eclectic music mix. As you wander from room to room by way of the labyrinthine, laser-lit corridors, you will stumble across expansive outdoor areas and cosy corners packed with cosmopolitan crowds. The Razzclub is the largest space, hosting big-name DJs like Maadraassoo or Legoteque as well as international indie bands like Arctic Monkeys, Foals and Two Door Cinema Club. The smaller Loft, Lolita and Pop Bar spaces groove with the grinding sounds of house, dance, garage, hip-hop and soul, while the Rex Room is reserved for more experimental beats. You can save a few euros at Razzmatazz by purchasing tickets online in advance.

The **Museu del Disseny de Barcelona** (Plaça de les Glòries Catalanes, 37, ajuntament. barcelona.cat/museudeldisseny/ en) is a thought-provoking celebration of the positive influence modern design has on our everyday lives. From here, it's a quick walk to some of the most progressive feats of modern architecture in Barcelona: the **Media-TIC Building (Carrer de Roc Boronat, 117, 22barcelona. com/content/view/41/427/ lang,en)**, which achieves its environmentally friendly ideals with automated panels that moderate the inside temperature, and the honeycombed **CNMC Building**, (Carrer de Bolívia, 56, cnmc.es), which incorporates the 19th-century Can Tiana textile factory.

Head for streets like **Carrer de la Selva de Mar, Carrer d'Espronceda** and **Carrer de Peru** to explore Poblenou's famous street art, or consider taking the **Steel Donkey street art bike tour** (see opposite page).

Take a detour on your walk down to the coast for a quick siesta in **Parque del Centro del Poblenou**, a five-hectare (12 acre) oasis of avant-garde sculptures, colourful plants and flower-draped tunnels. Don't miss the park's giant brick chimney, a remnant of the area's industrial past, and the **Los Nidos y Pozos del Cielo** (Nests and Wells of Heaven), an avant-garde sculptural space formed by a tapestry of vines and flowers.

POBLENOU LOCAL RECOMMENDS

Duncan Rhodes of Steel Donkey Bike Tours (steeldonkeybiketours.com) runs regular rides through Poblenou, seeking out gastronomic spots and street art along the way.

Poblenou Cemetery (Avinguda Icària, s/n): Tombs in this cemetery are stacked one on top of the other, giving it an intriguing aspect that makes it feel like a library of the deceased.

Plaça de les Glòries Catalanes (Plaça de les Glòries Catalanes, 10): Intended by Barcelona's influential urban planner Ildefons Cerda to be the city's central point, this space is home to the Torre Glòries (Torre Agbar), the Museu del Disseny and the revamped **Encants Vells Market** (*see* p. 094), making it shine with a new light.

Poblenou's beaches (Bogatell Beach and Marbella Beach): Poblenou borders the sea all along its eastern side, where you will find some of the city's best beaches. If lounging on the sands of Bogatell or Marbella feels too quiet, head to **Base Nautica** (Avinguda del Litoral, basenautica. org) and hire kayaks, paddleboards or windsurfing equipment.

Rambla del Poblenou: This main road through the heart of the district is full of tapas bar terraces, perambulating pensioners and school kids on kick scooters, and is much nicer than La Rambla proper.

Parc de Diagonal Mar (Carrer de Llull, 362): Designed with sustainability in mind, the snaking tubes that gird this space irrigate its rich ecosystems with groundwater, allowing plant life to thrive. There's more than a nod to Gaudí in the decorative features, whilst a children's play area provides some fun.

Eixample (extension) was the first neighbourhood developed after the city's medieval ramparts were knocked down in the 1850s, split into two parts: Dreta de l'Eixample (Eixample Right) and Esquerra de l'Eixample (Eixample Left). It was designed to be different from the Old Town, with broad, sunlit avenues that invite walkers to take a lengthy stroll.

This grid's designer, Ildefons Cerdà, dreamed of making life better for everyone, but his vision inevitably attracted the city's rich. Dreta de l'Eixample became an aspirational neighbourhood, with busy Passeig de Gràcia as one of its most desirable streets. It's where you'll find Gaudí's iconic Casa Batlló and Casa Milà (La Pedrera) as well as high-end boutiques, and fine restaurants.

SHOP
1 Janina Lencería
2 Mar de Cava
3 Loewe

SHOP, EAT AND DRINK
4 Santa Eulalia
5 Rambla de Catalunya

EAT AND DRINK
6 Monvinic
7 El Sifó d'en Garriga

DRETA DE L'EIXAMPLE

HOTEL CASA FUSTER

VILA DE GRÀCIA

CASA COMALAT

Font de la Palangana

AVINGUDA DIAGONAL

DIAGONAL

AVINGUDA DIAGONAL

CARRER DE ROGER DE LLÚRIA

CARRER DEL BRUC

CARRER DE MALLORCA

Room Mate Carla Hotel

MAR DE CAVA

BALUARD BAKERY

PALAU ROBERT

L5

Hotel Omm

Hotel Actual

CARRER DE PROVENÇA

Font de la Granota

L3

JARDINS DE PALAU ROBERT

DIAGONAL

Fundació Suñol

Next To Hotel

CARRER DE PAU CLARIS

CARRER DE VALÈNCIA

CASA MILÀ (LA PEDRERA)

CARRER DEL ROSSELLÓ

SANTA EULALIA

PASSEIG DE GRÀCIA

ALMA HOTEL

LA DRETA DE L'EIXAMPLE

BOCA CHICA COCKTAIL BAR

Murmuri Boutique Hotel

MAURI

LASARTE

Hotel Majestic

Museu Egipci de Barcelona

CARRER D'ARAGÓ

JANINA LENCERÍA

CARRER DE PROVENÇA

RAMBLA DE

HOTEL CONDES DE BARCELONA

RAMBLA DE CATALUNYA

PROVENÇA

L'EIXAMPLE

Olivia Balmes Hotel

PASSEIG DE GRÀCIA

CASA BATLLÓ

CASA AMATLLER

Mandarin Oriental Hotel

LOEWE

CATALUNYA

S1 S2 S5 S55

L6 L7

VALÈNCIA

N

EL SIFÓ D'EN GARRIGA

CARRER DE MALLORCA

Hotel Balmes

CARRER DE BALMES

hcc taber

RAMBLA DE CATALUNYA

ANTIGA ESQUERRA DE L'EIXAMPLE

R2 R2 Nord R2 Sud R11 R13 R14 R15 R16

CARRER D'ARAGÓ

CARRER DE CENT

Hotel Continental Palacete

GALERIA TONI TÀPIES

Museu del Modernisme Barcelona (MMBCN)

MONVINIC

Plaça del Doctor Letamendi

CARRER DEL CONSELL

CARRER DE

Fundación Mapfre

TAKTIKA BERRI

Seminari Major Interdiocesà

Hotel Sansi Diputació

CARRER D'ARAGÓ

CARRER D'ARIBAU

0   100 m

CARRER DE LA DIPUTACIÓ DE

BALMES

L2

Axel Hotel

GARAGE BEER CO. BREWERY

Universitat de Barcelona

GRAN VIA DE LES CORTS CATALANES

1.

JANINA LENCERÍA
Carrer del Rosselló, 233
932 15 04 84
janinalenceria.com
Open Mon–Sat 10am–8.30pm
Metro: Diagonal

Founded by Janina Santacana
in the late 1950s, this
lingerie store is a treasured
institution for luxurious
underwear, nightwear
and swimwear. Janina's
daughter, Janina Olivella,
took over the business in
the '60s and later passed it
on to her daughter, Janina
Terés: three generations of
Janinas. Brands and styles
change with the seasons
and focus on contemporary
looks from Italian and French
designers like Palladini,
Lenny Niemeyer, Hanro and
La Perla. The addition of an
instore workshop means
that most pieces can be
customised. Be sure to check
out the Janina Born collection,
which is made to measure
and also available straight
off the racks. Janina stocks a
range of quality underwear
for men too.

LOCAL TIP
Take time out in nearby
Jardins del Palau Robert
(Passeig de Gràcia, 107),
a secret garden belonging
to a stately mansion-
turned-art exhibition
space. Bursting with
tropical plants and brightly
coloured parakeets, it is a
true inner-city oasis.

2.

MAR DE CAVA
Carrer de València, 293
934 58 53 33
mardecava.com
Open Mon–Sat 10.30am–2pm
& 4.30–8.30pm
Metro: Girona

Browsing in this combination design gallery and shop, housed in a 100-year-old apartment in a listed Modernist building, feels like shopping in someone's very well-decorated home. This creative space is owned by interior designer Mar Gômez and is a classic Eixample home, complete with mosaic floors and ornate vaulted ceilings. Delve into 500 square metres (5382 square feet) full of limited-edition homewares created by Mar and local brands like Boca de Lobo, Apparatu and Amarist. From minimalist sofas and retro mirrors to suitcase-friendly illustrations and playful bedding, you'll find objects full of contemporary Barcelona cool. Mar also runs regular workshops to inspire people to unleash their creative side. Ask her about her latest sessions and try your hand at illustration, sculpture or a spot of architecture.

3.

LOEWE

Passeig de Gràcia, 35
932 16 04 00
loewe.com/eur/en/women/
bags/barcelona
Open Mon–Sat 10am–8.30pm
Metro: Passeig de Gràcia

Dating back to 1846, this leather accessories specialist is one of Spain's oldest and most cherished brands. Although they now have stores all over the country, their Barcelona branch is arguably the most spectacular. It occupies the ground floor of the Modernista Casa Lleó Morera, designed by Catalan design pioneer Lluís Domènech i Montaner. The elegance of the facade's wrought-iron balconies and floral friezes is contrasted nicely by the interior's minimalist design, where the latest collection of men's and women's luxury bags and shoes sit on illuminated podiums as if they were precious artefacts. For 2000€ you can buy the brand's iconic bag for women, the Puzzle Bag, whilst smaller clutches and wallets start at around 500€. The men's range of shoes and backpacks are equally bright and funky, with pieces ranging between 350€ and 10,000€.

4.

SANTA EULALIA

Passeig de Gràcia, 93
932 15 06 74
santaeulalia.com
Open Mon–Sat 10am–8.30pm
Metro: Diagonal

This emporium of sartorial splendour has been dressing Barcelona's most glamorous men and women since 1843. The emphasis is very much on haute couture, with a broad selection of formal and informal attire from brands like Alexander McQueen, Tom Ford and Christian Louboutin. As one of the oldest design houses in Spain, Santa Eulalia also offers its own exclusive ready-to-wear collections, with everything from casual tees and shorts to V-necks and jackets. Men can splurge on bespoke tailoring, with suits measured, cut and crafted by professional in-house tailors.

Round off your shopping experience in the Champagne bar on the top floor, which features vintage Santa Eulalia posters and the air of an old-world Parisian cafe. They serve Mediterranean-inspired dishes like steamed salmon with gratinated potatoes alongside glasses of Louis Roederer bubbly, all on a sun-kissed outdoor terrace. It's an idyllic lunch spot, whether you plan on shopping here or not.

Antoni Gaudí's Casa Batlló (Passeig de Gràcia, 43) and Josep Puig i Cadafalch's Casa Amatller just next door are the wildly mismatched architectural gems that gave rise to the block's nickname, Illa de la Discòrdia (Block of Discord).

5

RAMBLA DE CATALUNYA

This pedestrianised boulevard runs parallel to famous Passeig de Gràcia, offering a kilometre-long stretch of shopping and dining. You'll find **Casa del Libro**, a cavernous bookstore with a vast selection of books in Spanish and Catalan, as well as a good selection in English. Browse the latest fashion at stores like **Pretty Ballerina**, **Misako** and **System Action**, or pick up homewares and trinkets at **Muy Mucho** and **Casa Viva**.

Grab a table at **El Racó** for perfect pizzas, fresh salads and satisfying pasta dishes. The old wine cellar of **La Bodegueta** dates back to 1940 and is a hidden gem offering traditional tapas and a huge selection of local wines and vermouth. For something more sophisticated, head to **Cinco Jotas Rambla** and explore seasonal farm-to-table dining and some of the best Iberian ham in the city. Finish with cocktails at the exuberant **Boca Chica Cocktail Bar**.

Keep in mind that the busy cafe terraces attract the city's notorious pickpockets, so be sure not to leave your bag hanging off the back of your chair or anywhere you can't see it.

6.

MONVINIC

Carrer de la Diputació, 249
932 72 61 87
monvinic.com
Open Mon 7–10.30pm,
Tues–Fri 1.30–3.30pm
(lunch) & 8–10.30pm (dinner),
Sat 7–10.30pm
Metro: Passeig de Gràcia

The lovechild of sommelier Isabelle Brunet and businessman Sergi Ferrer-Salat, Monvinic is one of the most raved-about wine bars in Europe. The cellar bulges with more than 10,000 varieties of wine from all over the world. Throw in its library of books about wine and a team of professional sommeliers, and it's the perfect place to brush up on your wine knowledge. The decor is sleek and stylish, nothing like Barcelona's old-world bodegas (wine shops). Mirrored walls, wine lists displayed on iPads and futuristic green lighting make it feel a bit like an intergalactic spaceship, but the prices remain pleasantly down to earth.

There's also a plush dining area where you can enjoy dishes like gnocchi with black truffle, langoustines in ravioli apple, and chargrilled meats. Ask to be seated on the peaceful internal terrace so you can enjoy the full experience.

EL SIFÓ D´EN GARRIGA

Carrer Consell de Cent, 308
932 15 72 15
Open Mon–Fri 8–12am,
Sat–Sun 9–12am
Metro: Passeig de Gràcia

This suave-but-casual cafe and tapas bar is a rose amongst many tourist-trapping thorns. Start your day with healthy breakfast smoothies, juices and yoghurts with fruit, as well as pastries and home-baked cakes (with plenty of vegetarian and gluten-free options). A blue Marzocco espresso machine adorns the polished concrete bar where the team grinds single-origin beans from local roasters Nomad Coffee. The made-to-order sandwiches (a rare thing in Barcelona) are perfect for a light lunch with a beer or a glass of vermouth. Tapas dishes draw on high-quality ingredients and are a treat at any time of day. Share a board of local cheeses and Iberian hams, as well as dishes like the green-pea hummus with mint, and potato salad with smoked Cantabrian sardines. Organic wines, Catalan craft beers and creative cocktails offer the perfect excuse to loiter. Outstanding value for money, especially considering its central location.

Take a leisurely stroll past Barcelona's most recognisable Modernist buildings. Start at the undulating **Casa Milà** (La Pedrera) (Provença, 261–265), designed by Barcelona's most famous son, Antoni Gaudí. It was built between 1906 and 1912 for Roser Segimon and her husband Pere Milà, who lived on one floor and rented out the rest to high society. Critics panned the design, nicknaming it La Pedrera ('The Quarry') due to its unpolished stone face. Take a tour of the building and visit the apartments. A little further down the street is Gaudí's **Casa Batlló** (Passeig de Gràcia, 43), or the House of Bones. Wealthy textile tycoon Josep Batlló wanted a trophy home for his family to live in and encouraged Gaudí to go wild with the building's renovation. The result was a truly fantastical property. Take a tour and explore the equally mystical interior, including the Noble Floor where the Batlló family lived until the 1950s. At both Casa Milà and Casa Batlló you can enjoy rooftop music shows in the evenings in summer.

Just a quick metro ride away is Antoni Gaudí's divine **Sagrada Familia** church (Carrer de Mallorca, 401) – an iconic symbol of Barcelona. A devoutly religious man, Gaudí gave up all other design projects to focus entirely on what he called the 'work of God'. He even moved into the building site so he could keep a close eye on its progress. Today, his body is buried in a crypt in the belly of the church.

Marwa Preston is the founder of Wanderbeak Tours (wanderbeak.com), which runs the Gourmet Gaudí food and architecture tour in Dreta de l'Eixample.

Mercat de La Concepció (Carrer de Aragó, 313): I love to wander through this local market with fresh fruit in hand, checking out the array of meats and cheeses before visiting the huge flower market located near the market's Carrer de Valencia entrance.

Palau Robert (Passeig de Gràcia, 107): This former private residence houses fascinating exhibitions ranging from photography to gastronomy. It's located right on busy Passeig de Gràcia and makes for a lovely break from the hustle and bustle of city life.

Passeig de Gràcia & Passeig de Sant Joan: Passeig de Gràcia is one of the most colourful streets in the city and is where the bourgeoisie lived in the Modernist era. I see something new every time I walk this street, which makes me fall in love with the city again.

Mauri (Carrer de Provença, 241): Open since 1929, this is a definite favourite for small breakfasts (usually a tortilla de patatas sandwich) and coffee. Every corner of this Modernist gem is full of interesting details and the smell of freshly baked pastry always makes it hard to leave.

Alma Hotel (Carrer de Mallorca, 271): The garden at the back of the hotel is a secret oasis in the middle of the city. I go here to catch up on work, meet colleagues or just for some me-time.

Hotel Condes de Barcelona (Passeig de Gràcia, 73): One of my favourite rooftops in the city! I love to come here in the evenings and listen to live music while I enjoy a drink and a light snack. Their tacos are incredible.

With its wealth of Modernist buildings, exclusive boutiques and trendy food spots, the 'left side of Eixample' is every bit as elegant as the Right. Its absence of big-name tourist attractions means it's the province of locals, lending it a more authentic feel.

Esquerra de l'Eixample has long been nicknamed 'Gaixample' due to its thriving LGBTQ community. More recently, it has also been dubbed 'Beerxample' in honour of its many craft beer bars, all within walking distance of each other. As dusk falls, the city's night owls and mixology lovers come to enjoy some of the city's most stylish cocktail bars.

ESQUERRA DE L'EIXAMPLE

24 JUN 8016

SHOP
1 The Avant

SHOP, EAT AND DRINK
2 Las Arenas

EAT
3 Brunch & Cake
4 DelaCrem

17

EAT AND DRINK
5 Disfrutar
6 NaparBCN
7 La Dama
8 Artte
9 BierCab

DRINK
10 Solange

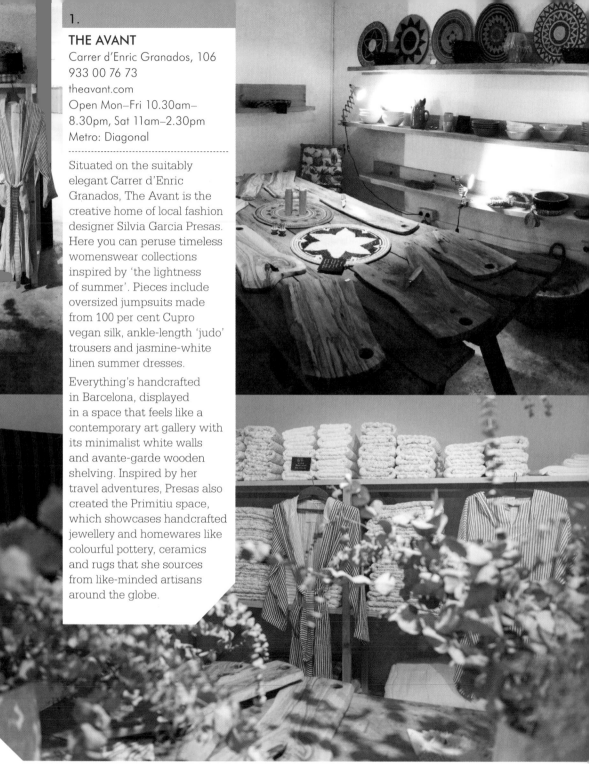

1.

THE AVANT

Carrer d'Enric Granados, 106
933 00 76 73
theavant.com
Open Mon–Fri 10.30am–
8.30pm, Sat 11am–2.30pm
Metro: Diagonal

Situated on the suitably elegant Carrer d'Enric Granados, The Avant is the creative home of local fashion designer Silvia Garcia Presas. Here you can peruse timeless womenswear collections inspired by 'the lightness of summer'. Pieces include oversized jumpsuits made from 100 per cent Cupro vegan silk, ankle-length 'judo' trousers and jasmine-white linen summer dresses.

Everything's handcrafted in Barcelona, displayed in a space that feels like a contemporary art gallery with its minimalist white walls and avante-garde wooden shelving. Inspired by her travel adventures, Presas also created the Primitiu space, which showcases handcrafted jewellery and homewares like colourful pottery, ceramics and rugs that she sources from like-minded artisans around the globe.

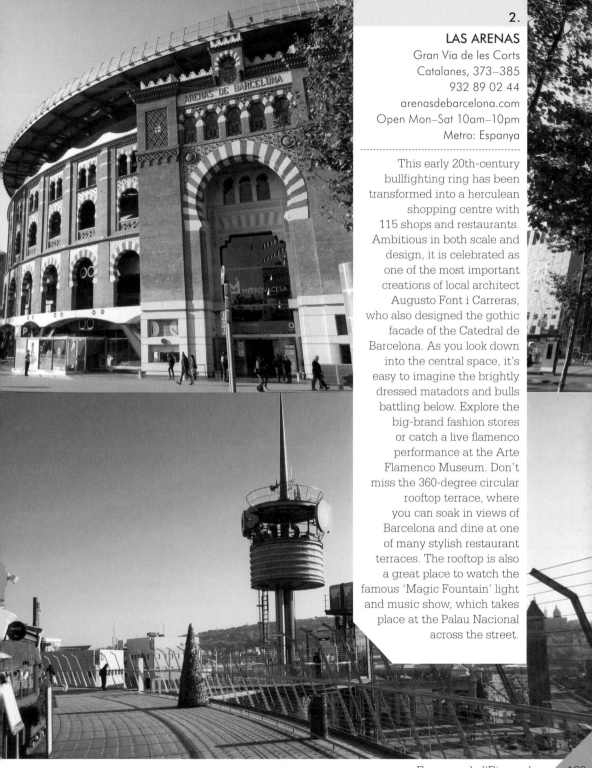

LAS ARENAS

Gran Via de les Corts
Catalanes, 373–385
932 89 02 44
arenasdebarcelona.com
Open Mon–Sat 10am–10pm
Metro: Espanya

This early 20th-century bullfighting ring has been transformed into a herculean shopping centre with 115 shops and restaurants. Ambitious in both scale and design, it is celebrated as one of the most important creations of local architect Augusto Font i Carreras, who also designed the gothic facade of the Catedral de Barcelona. As you look down into the central space, it's easy to imagine the brightly dressed matadors and bulls battling below. Explore the big-brand fashion stores or catch a live flamenco performance at the Arte Flamenco Museum. Don't miss the 360-degree circular rooftop terrace, where you can soak in views of Barcelona and dine at one of many stylish restaurant terraces. The rooftop is also a great place to watch the famous 'Magic Fountain' light and music show, which takes place at the Palau Nacional across the street.

3.

BRUNCH & CAKE

Carrer d'Enric Granados, 19
932 37 87 65
cupcakesbarcelona.com/shops-brunchcake
Open Mon–Sun 9am–10pm
Metro: Universitat

In a country where brunch is a relatively new concept, Barcelona is leading the way with cool cafes made for whiling away the morning as it turns into afternoon. Perched on a particularly leafy corner of Enric Granados, Brunch & Cake is bathed in sunlight – a pretty spot to linger over a coffee. As one of the pioneers of Barcelona's now booming brunch movement, it offers plenty of remedies to cure the effects of last night's fiesta. Indulge in waffles with poached eggs, bacon, cheese and truffle syrup, as well as French toast or pancakes with fresh fruit and maple syrup. Those on a health kick will find quinoa salads, smoothies and hearty granola and porridge options too. The homemade cakes go down beautifully with excellent organic coffee. They serve brunch all day, every day, so there's no need to rush.

DELACREM

Carrer d'Enric Granados, 15
930 04 10 93
delacrem.cat
Open Sun–Tues
9.30am–9.30pm,
Wed–Sat 9.30–12.30am
Metro: Universitat

This tiny corner cafe is where Italian-born Massimo Pignato crafts extra-creamy, gourmet 'gelato Italiano' (Italian-style ice-cream). Drawing on only the highest quality seasonal fruit, chocolate and nuts, it's no surprise that Pignato's sensational scoops are considered the best in Barcelona. Locals line up for flavours like roasted apple with cinnamon, dark chocolate with beer, and pistachio with hazelnut. If you're feeling especially adventurous, then be sure to ask about the latest frozen experiments – previous creations have included zesty flavours like cava sorbet, and an imaginative mojito ice-cream. There's also a range of gluten-free and vegan-friendly ice-creams to choose from, with sorbets ideal for the lactose intolerant. A fresh selection of cakes, pastries and sandwiches make for a quick, delicious lunch. The outside terrace is always packed out, but the shady street benches offer excellent opportunities for people watching.

5.

DISFRUTAR

Carrer de Villarroel, 163
933 48 68 96
en.disfrutarbarcelona.com
Open Tues–Sat 1–2.45pm
(lunch) & 8–9.45pm (dinner)
Metro: Hospital Clínic

Created by three Catalan chefs who earned their stripes at El Bulli, the much-lauded Catalonian restaurant that earned *The Restaurant Magazine*'s 'World's Best Restaurant' title no less than five times, Disfrutar is the ideal place to explore progressive Catalan cooking. Mateu Casañas, Oriol Castro and Eduard Xatruch create immensely imaginative dishes: think rose petals splashed with lychee and beads of gin, or amber-coated hazelnuts that you eat with your hands after coating them in 16-year-old Scotch.

The restaurant's narrow entranceway leads you past the huge open kitchen to a dining room featuring whitewashed walls and leafy plants taken from the nearby Costa Brava (Wild Coast). The service staff explain each dish and offer advice on how to eat them, while the sommeliers approach each wine pairing with unwavering skill. Tasting menus range from the 20-course Classic (110€) to the 26-course Gran Classic (150€) and the 'let's go all out' 31-course Disfrutar (180€).

6.

NAPARBCN

Carrer de la Diputació, 223
934 08 91 62
naparbcn.com
Open Tues–Wed 5pm–12am,
Thurs–Sat 12pm–2am
Metro: Universitat

With its edgy decor, onsite brewery and Michelin-starred head chef, NaparBCN is Beerxample's biggest and most impressive craft beer bar. This gastro brewpub is a collaboration between Spanish brewers Naparbier and chef Miquel Aldana, who employed local design legend Lázaro Rosa-Violán to create the dining space. The handsome dark-wood tables and tanned leather chairs are refined and sophisticated, while the rusted metal and skull-bedecked motorcycle hanging from one of the walls lend it a devil-may-care vibe. Brewer Beinat Gutierrez can typically be found in the open-fronted brewery, which features seven gargantuan fermentation tanks. There are 24 taps pouring everything from traditional dark stouts and pilsners to ultra-hoppy pale ales and red IPAs.

The food menu is equally impressive, featuring a range of classic Catalan flavours elevated with modern twists.

LOCAL TIP

Pop into Mercat del Ninot across the street to see where the chefs at Disfrutar find their inspiration and stock up on seasonal produce.

6.

6.

5.

7.

LA DAMA

Avinguda Diagonal, 423
932 09 63 28
la-dama.com
Open Mon–Sat 1.30–5pm
(lunch) & 8.30pm–3am (dinner)
Metro: Diagonal

Tucked inside the elegant, Gaudí-inspired Casa Sayrach building built in 1918, La Dama is arguably the most romantic French restaurant in town. A debonair doorman will usher you inside (so long as you have a reservation) to a speakeasy-inspired dining room with plush velvet wallpaper, dark wood panelling, crimson carpets and the flicker of candlelight. Every wall is adorned with works of art created especially for the restaurant. Parisian chef Edouard Deplus, who honed his craft at the Institut Paul Bocuse in France, blends the finesse of modern French cooking with the seasonality of Mediterranean ingredients. Explore flavours like beef carpaccio with pickles and chimichurri before moving on to braised beef with buttery potato purée or the mixed plato del mar seafood spread. Save room for the plump, fluffy desserts made by the in-house pastry chef. Don't leave without sampling something from the cocktail bar.

LOCAL TIP

The 1920s-inspired cocktail bar and live music venue Gatsby Barcelona is within stumbling distance of La Dama, offering a suitably lively place to kick on with a night of indulgence.

8.

ARTTE

Carrer de Muntaner, 83C
934 54 90 48
artte.es
Open Tues–Thurs 1pm–1am,
Fri–Sat 1pm–2am
Metro: Universitat

As the name hints ('art' plus 'tea'), this 400-square-metre (4306 square feet) space used to house a luxury tearoom, but now it pays homage to its past as an innovative restaurant and cocktail bar. Head mixologist Pablo Pelatt creates some of the most inventive cocktails in Barcelona and serves some of his colourful concoctions in ornate teapots in honour of the bar's tearoom roots. The Hombre Lobo (Werewolf) is a prime example: a mix of single-malt whisky with a sake and marigold infusion, shiitake-spiced tea and beetroot.

When it comes to food, chef Enric López's Latin American and South- East Asian heritage inspires dishes you won't find elsewhere in Barcelona, like squid drizzled with its ink and mango chutney, and ultra-slow-cooked crab served in a chilli bisque. The neon-lit dining space hosts sultry live jazz performances and DJ sets. The vintage telephones that adorn each table by the bar are connected, so if you fancy talking to the table next to you, just pick up the phone and give them a bell.

9.

BIERCAB

Carrer de Muntaner, 55
644 68 90 45
biercab.com/en
Open Mon–Thurs 12pm–12am,
Fri–Sat 12pm–2am,
Sun 5pm–12am
Metro: Universitat

With 30 draught beers on tap and fridges bulging with everything from Belgian lambics and saisons to American porters and IPAs, BierCab is a beer lover's dream. The decor, too, is rather special, with quirky wooden furnishings and funky lighting that look like they've been lifted out of an avant-garde art gallery. The selection of beers changes so frequently that it has to be displayed on huge screens, making it feel a little bit like drinking at a craft beer stock exchange. It's owned by Spanish brewers Naparbier, so there are plenty of local beers to try. Level out with one of their beautiful burgers made from 100 per cent Japanese wagyu beef. Try the Eixample Burger with provolone cheese and Iberian ham, or go with the eponymous BierCab Burger with foie gras, apple and tempura. Pop next door to the BierCab bottle shop where you can choose from 500 different beers to take home with you.

10

SOLANGE

Carrer d'Aribau, 143
931 64 36 25
facebook.com/
SolangeCocktails
Open Mon–Sun 6pm–2.30am
Metro: Hospital Clínic

With its vintage sofas, gold-flecked walls and ritzy chandeliers, Solange is one of Barcelona's most luxurious cocktail bars. James Bond fans will know that Solange is the name of one of the English spy's main love interests in *Casino Royale*, and in the spirit of all things 007, owner Alfredo Pernía and his team of highly-skilled mixologists dress impeccably in tailored suits. The cocktail list is even scented with aftershave by Tom Ford, the fashion icon responsible for designing Daniel Craig's suits in *Casino Royale*. Celebrating the classic cocktails of yesteryear, this is the place to indulge in timeless concoctions like old fashioneds, daiquiris and negronis. Or, for the full Bond experience, go for the house special Vesper Martini, which is the same gin-and-vodka concoction Bond quaffs – shaken, not stirred – to help him keep his poker face.

Antoni Gaudí's buildings may dominate Dreta de l'Eixample, but here on the Left Side there are plenty of lesser-known treasures to seek out. One of the most spectacular is **Casa Sayrach** (Avinguda Diagonal, 423–425), designed and built in 1918 by Catalan artist, poet and architect Manuel Sayrach. The elaborate lobby boasts bizarre, bone-like columns and spiraling arches that will transport you to the bottom of the ocean. Casa Sayrach isn't open to the general public, but guests dining at **La Dama** (see p. 128) can enjoy the dramatic lobby on their way inside. Right next door is **Casa Montserrat** (Carrer d'Enric Granados, 153), which Sayrach designed and built in 1926 for his wife Montserrat Xiprer.

Though the facade is sombre by comparison, it is still a work of great beauty – search for the little 'MiM' engravings, which mean 'Manuel and Montserrat'.

Don't miss **Parc de Joan Miró**, which sprawls out over four blocks. Resplendent with fragrant pine trees, evergreen oaks and pergolas, it's hard to believe this idyllic nook occupies a space that was once home to a slaughterhouse. It is named in honour of the iconic Catalan artist Joan Miró, whose evocative *Dona i Ocell* (Women and Bird) sculpture stands proudly in the park. Take a picnic and find a spot for a quick siesta – keep an eye out for colourful parakeets in the palm trees above.

Oscar Fuentes Loyola founded Zythos Beer Barcelona (Carrer del Rosselló, 185; zythosbeerbcn.com), a craft beer bottle shop where you can taste local and international brews and a selection of tapas.

Mercat del Ninot (Carrer Mallorca, 133): Unlike the more famous markets of La Boqueria and Mercado de Santa Caterina, this ancient market is mainly frequented by local residents and chefs. One of the best restaurants in the city, **Disfrutar** (*see* p. 126), pays homage to the market with its colourful ceramics and wrought-iron decor. The market also holds regular workshops, so it's a great place to learn about Catalan cooking.

Avinguda Diagonal: This is the longest street in Barcelona, stretching out diagonally across the entire city. It's packed with fashion boutiques, cafes and restaurants, as well as the architectural gem of **Casa Sayrach** (*see* opposite page). A cycle lane spans the entire length and if you follow it west, it will lead you to the beautiful Parc de Pedralbes.

Taktika Berri (Valencia, 169): This is my favourite place to gift my palate. The atmosphere at this Basque pintxo (a type of tapas) restaurant will take you to another space in time. The pintxos are hot and fresh and the txacolí (slightly sparkling white wine) is excellent.

Bodega Joan (Rosselló, 164): This is an great place for traditional Spanish food and a lively atmosphere. It's very Catalan: its name, Bodega Joan, in tribute to Joan Gamper, who founded of the Barcelona football club.

Often described as a village within the city, Gràcia started out as a small satellite town cut off from the rest of Barcelona. It's only a few metro stops from the city centre, but wandering its beautiful streets and plaças feels like escaping into another world.

Its sun-struck squares are among the prettiest in Barcelona, drawing bohemian types and families who congregate to gossip with their neighbours. Life here trundles along at a much slower pace than the rest of the city – at least it does until August, when residents celebrate the Festa Majór de Gràcia (Gràcia Festival). The cherry on Gràcia's cake is that it's located near Antoni Gaudí's fantastical Parc Güell, where you can see the architect's brazen mosaics in all their otherworldly glory.

GRÀCIA

24   JUN 8076

SHOP
1 El Piano Man
2 Be Concept Store

SHOP, EAT AND DRINK
3 Plaça del diamant

17

EAT AND DRINK
4 Gasterea
5 Syra
6 Nou Can Codina
7 La Pubilla
8 Café del Sol
9 Bar Virreina

DRINK
10 Cara B

0 — 100 m

SANT JOAN
DE GRÀCIA

CARRER DEL ROBÍ

CARRER DE VERDÍ

CARRER D'ASTÚRIES

CARRER DE L'OR

CARRER DEL TORRENT D'EN VIDALET

CARRER DE SANT LLUÍS

CARRER DE MONTMANY

CARRER BRUNIQUER

CARRER DE JOAN BLANQUES

CARRER DE JOAN

CARRER DEL TORRENT DE LES FLORS

CARRER DE

CARA B ○

○ **BAR
VIRREINA**

GASTEREA
⊕ CINE
VERDI

○ **PLAÇA
DEL
DIAMANT**

CARRER DE LA PERLA

○ **EL PIANO
MAN**

CARRER DE VERDI

CARRER DE TORRIJOS

CARRER DE RAMÓN Y CAJAL

GRÀCIA

Teatreneu ■

CARRER DE TEROL

CARRER DE RAMÓN Y CAJAL

CARRER DE TORRIJOS

TRAVESSERA DE GRÀCIA

CARRER DEL MONTSENY

CARRER DE JAÉN

Centre Artesà ■
Tradicionarius

CARRER DE ROS DE OLANO

CARRER DEL PLANETA

**CAFÉ
DEL SOL** ○

CARRER DEL CANÓ

CARRER DE DELS DESEMPARATS

CARRER DE LA MARE DE DÉU

Mercat de
l'Abaceria

CARRER DE SIRACUSA

CARRER DE PUIGMARTÍ

GRÀCIA

SYRA ○

CARRER DE TORDERA

TRAVESSERA

CARRER DEL PENEDÈS

**VILA DE
GRÀCIA**

CARRER DEL TORRENT DE L'OLLA

CARRER DEL PROGRÉS

N

Plaça de la
Vila de Gràcia

CARRER DE SANT DOMÈNEC

CARRER DE GOYA

CARRER DE MARTÍNEZ DE LA ROSA

CARRER DE FRANCISCO GINER

**TO
LA PUBILLA**
(SEE MAP LEFT)

CARRER DE SANT PERE MÀRTIR

CARRER DE MOZART

**NOU CAN
CODINA** ○

CARRER GRAN DE GRÀCIA

LLUÍS ANTÚNEZ

DE BONAVISTA

**BE
CONCEPT
STORE**

CARRER DE

CARRER DE LA RIERA DE SANT MIQUEL

L3

HOTEL
CASA
FUSTER

CARRER D'APEL·LES FENOSA

CARRER

CARRER DE CÓRSEGA

Jardins de
Salvador
Espriu

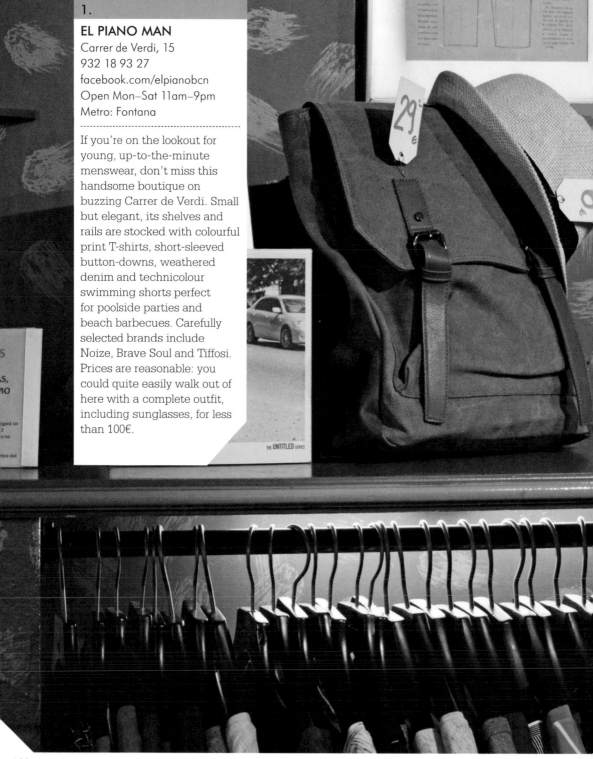

1.

EL PIANO MAN

Carrer de Verdi, 15
932 18 93 27
facebook.com/elpianobcn
Open Mon–Sat 11am–9pm
Metro: Fontana

If you're on the lookout for young, up-to-the-minute menswear, don't miss this handsome boutique on buzzing Carrer de Verdi. Small but elegant, its shelves and rails are stocked with colourful print T-shirts, short-sleeved button-downs, weathered denim and technicolour swimming shorts perfect for poolside parties and beach barbecues. Carefully selected brands include Noize, Brave Soul and Tiffosi. Prices are reasonable: you could quite easily walk out of here with a complete outfit, including sunglasses, for less than 100€.

LOCAL TIP
Pop in to the Mercat de l'Abaceria (Travessera de Gràcia, 186), one of the most authentic neighbourhood food markets in Barcelona, and pick up a few treats to take home with you.

2.

BE CONCEPT STORE

Carrer de Bonavista, 7
932 18 89 49
bethestore.com
Open Mon–Sat 10am–9pm
Metro: Diagonal

Prepare to discover a bold new world of creative design here, from uber-hipster fashion and wacky travel accessories to kitchen gadgets and unusual gifts. The store is bright, expansive and feels a bit like a contemporary design exhibition. Browse for neon-pink flamingo lamps, shamanic tea sets and colourful photography books. Or treat your eyes to handcrafted Raen sunglasses from California and a pair of the latest kicks from Vans, Nike or Puma. No matter what your budget, you're sure to find something that stirs your imagination.

3.

PLAÇA DEL DIAMANT

Gràcia is renowned for its many beautiful squares, but this unassuming little nook harbours the most fascinating history of them all. It was built in 1860 on land belonging to jewel magnate Josep Rossell, hence the name 'Diamond Square'. As with many of the squares throughout the area, an underground air raid shelter was constructed here during the Spanish Civil War. Unlike other shelters, most of which no longer exist, Plaça del Diamant's is perfectly intact. The **Gràcia History Workshop** will give you a guided tour, if you book your spot ahead. The square was made even more famous by Catalan writer Mercè Redoreda i Gurgui, who immortalised it in her 1962 novel *La Plaça del Diamant* about the struggles of young women growing up in the square during the Spanish Civil War. A sculpture here called **La Colometa** ('Little Dove') depicts the desperation of the book's main character.

Be sure to pop into **Könos Natural Taste** to indulge in freshly baked cakes, pastries and pizzas, as well as some of the best Italian-style gelato in the city. **Cafe Diamant** has a cosy outdoor terrace and is the perfect place to absorb the square's history.

LOCAL TIP

Stroll down to the Jardins de Salvador Espriu, where you can relax on a bench under the palm trees and soak in the colourful Modernist architecture. Five-star Hotel Casa Fuster (Passeig de Gràcia, 132) is an indulgent visual feast.

4.

GASTEREA

Carrer de Verdi, 39
932 37 23 43
facebook.com/pages/
Gasterea/167705123268614
Open Mon–Tues & Thurs
6.30pm–12am, Fri 6.30pm–
1am, Sat 12pm–12am,
Sun 6.30pm–12am
Metro: Fontana

Surrounded by a host of beautiful boutiques on a particularly stylish stretch of Carrer de Verdi, Gasterea's fresh and tasty pintxos (a type of tapas from northern Spain) are perfect for a post-shopping-spree bite. Elbow your way past the locals and squeeze onto a seat at the bar, where you can help yourself to traditional pintxos like gildas (skewers with pickled peppers, olives and anchovies), morcilla (black sausage) with a quail's egg, and grilled brochetas de gambas (prawn skewers) with garlic. See it all away with a bottle of txakoli, a slightly bubbly white wine enjoyed in the Basque Country, or try some traditional Basque cider. The staff are friendly and attentive, but don't be afraid to wave them over during busy periods. They come by from time to time and offer you pintxos directly from the kitchen – these are the freshest and tastiest, so be sure to grab 'em while they're hot.

SYRA

Carrer se la Mare de Déu
dels Desamparats, 8
666 72 07 43
syracoffee.com
Open Mon–Fri 8am–6pm,
Sat 8am–7pm
Metro: Fontana

Hidden on a nondescript side
street in the heart of Gràcia,
this tiny speciality coffee
shop was the first place in
Barcelona to specialise in
quality coffee to go (though
there is space to hang out in,
too). It's the creation of Yassir
Rais, a young architect and
entrepreneur who designed
this pint-sized space himself
using reclaimed materials and
a crisp white-on-wood colour
palette. It looks like something
straight out of the cool design
magazines he leaves out for
customers to peruse while
waiting for their caffeine fix.
A range of suitably artisanal
homemade cakes, doughnuts
and pastries make the perfect
companions, though you're
sure to make a friend or
two once you've settled in
with the regulars.

6.

NOU CAN CODINA

Carrer del Torrent de l'Olla, 20
935 16 15 84
facebook.com/cancodina
Open Mon–Sun 12pm–12am
Metro: Diagonal

Dating back to 1931, Can Codina is one of the oldest tapas bars in Gràcia and was renovated in 2016 to ensure it's in better shape than ever. The rustic decor has been left largely untouched: customers still sit on Parisian-style wooden chairs and dine at wrought-iron-and-marble tables. The huge granite bar remains, but now it holds countless craft beers from Catalan brewers and boutique wines from local wineries that attract a younger, more cosmopolitan crowd. There's quite a buzz on Friday and Saturday nights, especially if they're screening the latest FC Barcelona football game. Enjoy traditional tapas like crispy croquettes, sizzling botifarra morcilla (spicy blood sausage) and patatas bravas (spicy potatoes) with a rich tomato salsa, and try the cargols (snails) if you're feeling adventurous. Nou Can Codina's 9.90€ menú del día (set lunch menu) is a budget traveller's dream.

LOCAL TIP
Visit the Gaudí-inspired Casa Comalat, designed by Salvador Valeri i Pupurull and built between 1906 and 1911. The elegant main facade (Avinguda Diagonal, 442) is a triumph of balconies and floral motifs, while the rear facade (Carrer de Còrsega, 316) is equally impressive.

7.

LA PUBILLA

Plaça de la Llibertat, 23
932 18 29 94
facebook.com/lapubilla.gracia
Open Mon 8.30–5pm,
Tues–Fri 8.30–12am,
Sat 9am–12am
Metro: Fontana

The key to good Spanish cooking – or, in this case, Catalan cooking – lies in the freshness and quality of its ingredients. So it's no surprise that La Pubilla, an unassuming little Catalan restaurant tucked away behind Mercat de la Llibertat, is a delicious place to delve into local market cuisine. Chef Alexis Peñalver's bargain 16€ menú del día (set lunch menu) has become a firm favourite with local foodies and includes three courses, bread and wine (or beer). Dishes change with the seasons, but you can expect the likes of bacalao (salted cod) and hearty faves a la catalana (a stew of broad beans with crispy bacon and blood sausage). Desserts are refreshingly stripped back and make the most of whatever fruit is in season.

The menú del día is only available Tuesday through Friday, so reserve a table for one of three time slots (1.30, 2.30 or 3.30).

8.

CAFÉ DEL SOL

Plaça del Sol, 16
932 37 14 48
facebook.com/Cafe-del-Sol-414923205245387
Open Mon–Sun 11–2.30am
Metro: Fontana

Located in the sun-drenched Plaça del Sol (Sun Square), this is a proper locals' bar that epitomises the laid-back vibe that makes this neighbourhood inviting. Service is slow, but it's always friendly. While the inside space is a little worn, the terrace out the front is one of the area's most coveted places to sit and sip a cerveza (beer) or two. Come for an informal lunchtime feast and nibble on tapas like choricitos (little sausages) cooked in red wine, premium-quality olives and satiating patatas bravas (spicy potatoes). Sip on the house-special mojitos, served in giant goblets with fistfuls of fresh mint, to see why the regulars keep coming back. This is a popular square for some of the city's best buskers, so if you're lucky you might even get to enjoy a free concert while you're here.

8.

8.

8.

7.

7.

8.

9.

BAR VIRREINA

Plaça de la Virreina, 1
934 15 32 09
virreinabar.com
Open Mon–Fri 9–1am,
Sat–Sun 10–12am
Metro: Fontana

Plaça de la Virreina is the neighbourhood's prettiest square, home to Bar Virreina's tree-shaded terrace – the ultimate place from which to soak in the beauty. The tapas menu is excellent (try the nachos), but it's more of a 'couple of drinks and something to nibble on' kind of place. The beer's cold, and they have a solid selection of Spanish wines and vermouth to enjoy while you enjoy views of the imposing Parròquia de Sant Joan Baptista de Gràcia (Sant Joan church) and revel in the romantic ambience. Plaça de la Virreina is popular with local families, who come to kick a football around and race their scooters to the steps of the church. In many ways, going for a drink or two at Bar Virreina is the best way to immerse yourself in Gràcia's village vibe.

10.

LOCAL TIP

Parròquia de Sant Joan Baptista de Gràcia (Carre de la Santa Creu, 2) dates back to 1878. Historians believe its chapel was designed by Antoni Gaudí, and that he used the project to test ideas he had for La Sagrada Familia.

CARA B

Carrer del Torrent de les Flors, 36
932 22 55 46
facebook.com/cara.bbarcelona
Open Mon–Thurs 6pm–2.30am, Fri–Sat 6pm–3.30am
Metro: Joanic

Strict noise regulations means it's nigh on impossible for small bars in Barcelona to get licences to play live music, but Cara B is one of the lucky few. It's a tiny space – the kind where you can leave your friends to get a drink from the bar and still be able to keep track of the conversation. Its diminutive scale makes for extremely intimate live shows, with local musicians literally stepping out of the audience and onto the stage to perform soul-stirring acoustic sets. As well as being known as one of Gràcia's best live music venues, Cara B is adored for its huge selection of craft beers, ranging from local micro-batch brews to old Belgian stalwarts.

Don't miss the newly opened **Casa Vicens** (Carrer de les Carolines, 20, casavicens.org), which was Antoni Gaudí's first-ever commissioned house design project. With its colourful ceramic facade and ornate Moorish influences, it is widely regarded as an important historical prelude to the Catalan Modernista architecture movement. Gaudí's emblematic **Park Güell** (Carrer d'Olot, parkguell.es) is also within easy reach. Note that, although they have started charging to explore the main terrace area, you can see most of the park without paying a cent. Walk over to the **Carmel Bunkers** (MUHBA Turó de la Rovira, Carrer de Marià Lavèrnia), the government's anti-aircraft battery that inspired the area's nickname, Barrio de Canons. The canons are gone, but the views over the city are unrivalled.

Step back in time at **Cine Verdi** (Carrer de Verdi, 32, cines-verdi.com/barcelona), an old-world cinema that screens European arthouse films. It's also one of the best places to watch the latest blockbusters in English.

Misty Barker is a tour guide at Devour Tours (devourbarcelonafoodtours. com), a local company offering gourmet food tours in Gràcia.

Festa Major de Gràcia: This vibrant explosion of colourful street decorations adorning the neighbourhood takes over Gràcia for one week each year in August. I love to stroll the streets and soak up the atmosphere and excitement.

Plaça de la Vila de Gràcia: Sit at one of the many outdoor cafe terraces and enjoy a glass of cava while watching the world go by. This emblematic square is home to the town hall and the famous clock tower. It's where historic and modern-day Gràcia meet, seamlessly.

Bodea Cal Pep (Carrer de Verdi, 141): Each time I enter this beautiful old bodega (wine shop and bar), I'm instantly happier. It has old-school vibes and charm with some of the best vermouth around. Grab a seat with the locals and you may even be lucky enough to witness a Catalan sing-song while you're there.

Pastisseria Ideal (Carrer Gran de Gràcia, 207): Hidden inside its old sweet-shop-style doors lies a beautifully traditional coffee shop. Perch in the back room with a good book, strong coffee and a fresh pastry.

Resting at the foot of the Serra de Collserola mountains, ultra-exclusive Sarrià-Sant Gervasi is known as Barcelona's Zona Alta (Upper Zone). With beautifully manicured gardens, parks and squares, and a wealth of small boutiques, cafes and restaurants, it is typically described as being the most pijo (posh) of the city's neighbourhoods.

Sarrià-Sant Gervasi is home to many of Barcelona's rich and glamorous, including FC Barcelona footballer Gerard Piqué and his megastar partner Shakira. Despite the concentration of wealth, local life tends to be somewhat low-key. Made up of multiple villages that were swallowed up as the city expanded, its broad streets feel a world away from tourist-thronged Old Town.

24   JUN 8016

SHOP
1 Nonchalante

SHOP AND EAT
2 Foix de Sarrià

SHOP, EAT AND DRINK
3 Plaça de La Concòrdia
4 L'illa Diagonal

17

EAT AND DRINK
5 Bar Tomàs
6 Tram-Tram
7 Bangkok Cafe

DRINK
8 Gimlet
9 The Sutton Club

SARRIÀ-SANT GERVASI

TRAM-
TRAM

ESGLÉSIA
DE SANT
VICENÇ
DE SARRIÀ

REMA
ELISENDA

SARRIÀ

FOIX DE
SARRIÀ

BAR
TOMÀS

Hotel
Eurostars
Anglí

Cementiri
de Sarrià

LES TRES
TORRES

200 m

LES TRES
TORRES

SARRIÀ-
SANT
GERVASI

SANT GERVASI-
BONANOVA

SANT
GERVASI-
GALVANY

LA BONANOVA

Hotel
Catalonia
Castellnou

TO
GIMLET AND THE
SUTTON CLUB
(SEE MAP LEFT)

SARRIÀ

Hotel
HUSA
Pedralbes

NONCHALANTE

Jardins de
Vil·la Cecília

Jardins de
Vil·la
Amèlia

CHIRINGUITO
SANTA
AMELIA

PASSEIG DE MANUEL GIRONA

Plaça
del Mirall
de Pedralbes

Arenas
Atiram
Hotel

Jardins
de Joan
Vinyolí

Jardins
del Camp
de Sarrià

Jardins
d'Olga
Sacharoff

Jardins
de Piscines
i Esports

Jardins
del Doctor
Samuel
Hahnemann

L'ILLA

AVINGUDA DE SARRIA

DIAGONAL

NUMÀNCIA

L'ILLA
DIAGONAL

Hilton
Barcelona

AC Hotel
Victoria
Suites

PEDRALBES

PAVELLONS
DE LA FINCA
GÜELL

MARIA
CRISTINA

AVINGUDA
DIAGONAL

PLAÇA
DE LA
CONCÒRDIA

Hotel
NH Barcelona
Les Corts

Parc
de les
Corts

JARDINES DEL
PALACIO DE
PEDRALBES

PIUS XII

El Corte
Inglés

Jardins
de Jaume
Vicens
i Vives

Roca
Barcelona
Gallery

PALAU REIAL

Princesa Sofia
Gran Hotel

LA MATERNITAT
I SANT RAMON

LES
CORTS

LES
CORTS

08028
Apartments

LES
CORTS

BANGKOK
CAFE

PLAÇA DEL
CENTRE

Cementiri
de Les Corts

Jardins
de la
Maternitat

NH
Barcelona
Stadium
Hotel

Plaça
del Sòl
de Baix

CAMP
NOU

1.

NONCHALANTE

Carrer de Manuel de Falla, 13
932 05 91 40
nonchalante.es
Open Mon–Fri 10am–2.30pm
& 4.30–8.30pm, Sat 10am–
3pm & 5–8pm
Metro: Maria Cristina

Tucked away on a leafy side street, this petite shrine to female fashion is full of unique finds. The shop is the creation of local fashionista Laia Martinell, who sources her contemporary collection from French, Italian and Spanish brands like Soeur, Momoní and LOA. Browse the rails for hand-sewn cotton shirts that evoke the wistful styles of the French Riviera, T-shirts cut from organic cotton with bold and irreverent designs, and ethereal skirts and dresses made with 100 per cent gauze cotton. Martinell also stocks a colourful range of handbags and totes, all perfect for beach days or party nights. There's something for all budgets, whether you're looking for a new outfit or a fashionable Barcelona keepsake.

2.

FOIX DE SARRIÀ

Carrer Major de Sarrià, 57
932 03 07 14
foixdesarria.com
Open Mon–Sun 8am–9pm
Metro: Sarrià (FGC)

Founded by Josep Foix i Ribera in 1886, the pastry artists at Foix de Sarrià are long-time masters of oven-baked decadence. Perched on a corner plot and filled with traditional glass cabinets, it's impossible to walk past without stopping. The picture-perfect cakes are generously adorned with fresh fruit and piped with cream, while the chocolate truffles and classic bonbons are a treat for even the most dedicated chocoholics. Given its old-world charm, it's no wonder that members of the Spanish royal family shop here. Foix's limited-edition chocolate boxes, embellished with paintings by iconic Catalan artists, make for beautiful souvenirs and gifts. Pick up a selection of baked goods and stroll to tree-fringed Plaça de Sarrià for an impromptu picnic.

1.

1.

2.

2.

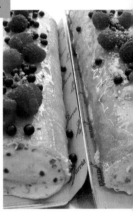

1.

1.

3.

PLAÇA DE LA CONCÒRDIA

Tucked away in quiet, residential Les Corts is one of Barcelona's best-kept secrets. Hidden well off the tourist trail, this leafy square provides a charming insight into local life. Families linger on the cafe terraces, their children running riot, while churchgoers flood in and out of the ornate **Santa Maria del Remei** parish church (founded in 1836). Enjoy giant gin and tonics at **Rabbar**, or head to the Parisian-looking **Fragments Cafe** for seasonal Spanish dishes (the 14.50€ set lunch menu is outstanding) – ask to be seated in their internal courtyard for a little extra romance. You'll find excellent tapas and boutique wines at the ever-popular **El Maravillas**.

The mighty **L'illa** shopping mall is just a five-minute stroll away, making this idyllic square perfect for a post- or pre-spree pit stop.

LOCAL TIP
Seek out Passatge de Tubella and explore one of Barcelona's cutest streets. Lined with little two-storey houses (a rarity in Barcelona) complete with gardens and inner courtyards, it feels very much like a traditional terraced street in Britain.

4.

L'ILLA DIAGONAL

Avinguda Diagonal, 557
934 44 00 00
lilla.com
Open Mon–Sat 10am–9.30pm
Metro: Les Corts

Inspired by the skyscrapers of New York City, this gleaming mega-mall sprawls out over 35,000 square metres (376,737 square feet) and houses more than 170 shops, bars and restaurants. One of the most exclusive shopping destinations in Barcelona, it's packed with big brand fashion stores like Zara, Bershka, Primark and Stradivarius. You'll also find every type of sportswear imaginable at the huge Decathlon store, and the latest electronics and entertainment at FNAC. El Corte Inglés, Spain's beloved department store company, also has a branch here and is the place to go if you're after cosmetics from brands like Mac, Rituals and The Body Shop. Restaurants are mainly chains, but you can enjoy decent seafood, traditional Spanish tapas, Mexican burritos and sushi. All in all, this is an excellent place to drop of few euros.

5.

BAR TOMÀS

Carrer Major de Sarrià, 49
932 03 10 77
eltomasdesarria.com
Open Mon–Sat 12–4pm
(lunch) & 6–10pm (dinner)
Metro: Sarrià (FGC)

This informal tapas bar is famous for serving the best patatas bravas (spicy potatoes) in Barcelona – in a city where every bar and restaurant dreams of bravas stardom, that's saying something. The potatoes here are cut more like chunky British chips than Spain's typically cubed ones, but the real key to their success is the garlic-laden aioli and spicy tomato salsa: they're so well renowned that the recipes are highly guarded secrets. Pop in for a laid-back lunch and enjoy your bravas with a few other tapas, or indulge in one of the hearty, rustic platos combinados (mixed plates). Do as the locals do and wash it all down with a few cañas (tiny tankards of ice-cold draught beer). Come early to secure a spot on the coveted outdoor terrace, or grab one of the retro formica tables by the bar and watch the place burst into life.

LOCAL TIP

Stroll up and down Carrer Major de Sarrià (in Sarrià) to find traditional stores that have been run by multiple generations.

4.

5.

4.

6.

TRAM-TRAM

Carrer Major de Sarrià, 121
932 04 85 18
tram-tram.com
Open Tues 1.30–3.30pm,
Wed–Sat 1.30–3.30pm (lunch)
& 9–10.45pm (dinner)
Metro: Sarrià (FGC)

Tucked at the narrow end of Carrer Major de Sarrià, a little way out of the main commercial hubbub, Tram-Tram offers affordable fine dining and a chance to escape the crowds. Run by husband-and-wife duo chef Isidre Soler and maître d' Reyes Lizan, this elegant restaurant occupies an old townhouse and unfolds through a series of intimate rooms. Don't miss the internal courtyard, filled with fragrant pot plants and vertical gardens. The 29€ three-course lunch menu, served Tuesday to Friday, offers unbeatable value for money, especially in this part of town, and includes Catalan-inspired dishes like duck salad with Iberian ham, freshly grilled fish of the day, coconut ice-cream with candied fruits as well as bread and wine. Splurge on the 90€ Festival tasting menu and chef Soler will dazzle you with a seemingly endless parade of dishes that include multiple desserts and cheese boards. If the Festival is a stretch, try the excellent 47.50€ seasonal tasting menu.

7.

BANGKOK CAFE

Carrer d'Evarist Arnús, 65
933 39 32 69
facebook.com/Bangkokcafe-
Barcelona-110153849007383
Open Mon–Wed 8–11.30pm,
Thurs–Sun 1–3.30pm (lunch) &
8–11.30pm (dinner)
Metro: Plaça del Centre

The Spanish don't really *do* spicy food, making this tiny temple of Thai gastronomy something of a hidden gem. Gold-framed photographs of Thailand's royal family adorn the walls and chintzy chandeliers loom from the ceiling. It's an informal, haphazard (veering on kitch) sort of vibe: the tables and chairs are jammed in next to each other, so you can't help but eavesdrop on your neighbours. It's always packed out, so it seems like no one minds. Order steamed prawns, beef dumplings and a sweet-and-spicy papaya salad, followed by picture-perfect pad thai and a suitably strong curry. The staff, all Thai, are warm and inviting – they will make sure you're always furnished with a frosty bottle of Singha beer. The prices aren't quite street hawker low, but you can eat well without spending much more than 15€ to 20€. It's best to make a reservation, but if you don't mind waiting, ask if you can hang out in the little garden until a table becomes free.

8.

GIMLET

Carrer de Santaló, 46
932 01 53 06
drymartiniorg.com/locales/
gimlet-v2
Open Mon–Wed 6pm–1am,
Thurs 6pm–2.30am,
Fri–Sat 6pm–3am
Metro: La Bonanova (FGC)

Legendary mixologist Javier de las Muelas has built a global empire of classy cocktail bars over the last few decades, but Gimlet, founded in 1979, will always be the original. With its smooth jazz soundtrack, sultry black-on-red colour palette and mahogany bar, it is a benchmark of timeless style and sophistication. Even so, the vibes are casual; you don't have to wear a tuxedo or arrive in a limo, which is refreshing for such a fancy venue. The magic here is in the details, from the branded cocktail shakers and napkins to the specially made Schweppes mixers that bear Javier's signature. It's located well off the tourist trail and is definitely a local favourite. Many come for the first-class service as much as the tasty concoctions. All of the cocktails are beautifully prepared – the Old Fashioned is a work of art – and served in elegant crystalware. You can't leave without trying the house-special Gimlet: a balanced fusion of premium-quality gin and lime juice.

THE SUTTON CLUB

Carrer de Tuset, 13
667 43 27 59
thesuttonclub.com
Open Mon–Thurs 12–5.30am,
Fri–Sat 12–6am
Metro: Diagonal

The Sutton Club is a homing beacon for the local glitterati, making this one of the wildest (and most expensive) nights out in Barcelona. Behind its glowing fuchsia facade is a decadent space filled with luxury sofas and cordoned-off VIP areas, where FC Barcelona superstar footballers like Leo Messi and Gerard Piqué come to celebrate their victories. The party starts warming up around 1am and is positively bouncing by 2, full of beautiful people who look like they've stepped straight off the catwalk. The stage hosts big-name artists like Sean Paul, Calvin Harris and Pitbull. Remember to pack something fancy to wear or you may not get past the surly doormen. Go to the website and put your name on the guest list for free entry or you'll pay 20€ at the door.

Follow in the footsteps of football's biggest legends with the **Camp Nou experience and museum visit** (Carrer d'Aristides Maillol, 12, fcbarcelona.com/tour). Home to FC Barcelona since 1957, this is Spain's largest football stadium and the spiritual home of what many claim to be the greatest soccer team of all time. Explore the locker rooms, trace the tunnel out to the pitch, and don't leave without giving one of the trophies in the museum a good-luck kiss.

For a breath of fresh air and a chance to stretch your legs, take a stroll through the verdant **Parc de Pedralbes**. Here you can walk among towering cypress trees and manicured flowerbeds, and visit the **Pedralbes Royal Palace** where the Spanish royal family used to stay when they came to Barcelona. Antoni Gaudí also left his mark here with a gorgeous vine-strangled pergola and Hercules-inspired water fountain. Just across the street you can also visit Gaudí's **Pavellons de la Finca Güell** (Avinguda de Pedralbes, 7, barcelonaturisme.com/wv3/en/page/607/pavellons-de-la-finca-guell), which flies way under most tourists' radars. If you have time, also check out the ancient **Monestir Pedralbes** (Baixada del Monestir, 9, monestirpedralbes.bcn.cat), where you can explore more than 700 years of Catalan history, art and culture.

Laia Martinell is the owner of **Nonchalante** (*see* p. 154), an independent boutique stocking the best selection of Italian, Spanish and French fashion brands.

Mercat Galvany (Carrer de Santaló, 65): Though not as famous as La Boqueria (see p. 039), Mercat Galvany maintains the soul of a local market. I love admiring its beautiful iron construction and buying fresh food that comes straight from the garden.

Sant Vicenç de Sarrià Church (Carrer Pinós, 10): This neoclassical church was built in 1781 by Josep Mas. Take a seat on one of the nearby terraces and sip local vermouth Morro Fi while taking in its ancient beauty.

Carretera de les Aigües (Funicular de Vallvidrera Station): On Sundays, I enjoy going to this natural 9.5-kilometre (5.9-mile) track at the foot of Collserola Natural Park. Sometimes I ride and sometimes I walk, but it is always nice for the impressive view of Barcelona and the fresh air. I love going for a vermouth afterwards at **Mirablau** or **Merbeyé** (both in Plaça del Dr. Andreu).

Plaça Molina: This little square with beautiful terraces is where locals hang out at the weekend. Indulge in a late lunch at **La Bodega** (Plaça Molina, 2) for a local meal with great service or **Casa Varela** (Plaça Molina, 4) for a fancier dining experience.

Wagokoro (Carrer de Regàs, 35): This authentic Japanese restaurant is a true hidden gem with healthy and delicious dishes. Don't miss the excellent sake.

Chiringuito Santa Amelia (Carrer de Santa Amelia): Situated in the Jardins de Amèlia Vil·la, this is a great place for a lazy Sunday lunch under the trees. Perfect for families or for anyone looking for tranquil moments in nature.

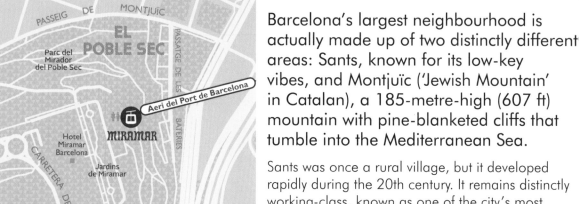

Barcelona's largest neighbourhood is actually made up of two distinctly different areas: Sants, known for its low-key vibes, and Montjuïc ('Jewish Mountain' in Catalan), a 185-metre-high (607 ft) mountain with pine-blanketed cliffs that tumble into the Mediterranean Sea.

Sants was once a rural village, but it developed rapidly during the 20th century. It remains distinctly working-class, known as one of the city's most down-to-earth neighbourhoods. Montjuïc is well known for its imposing stone fortress, the colossal Castell de Montjuïc (Montjuïc Castle). The area was transformed to host the 1929 International Exhibition and the 1992 Olympics. Its art galleries, museums and sports facilities are still in use and among Barcelona's most popular attractions.

24   JUN 8OT6

SHOP
1 CELLER DE GELIDA

SHOP AND EAT
2 BOMBONERIA PONS

EAT AND DRINK
3 LA TERE GASTROBAR
4 MARTINEZ
5 TERRAVINO
6 LA PARADETA
7 ADDIS ABEBA

17

DRINK
8 HOMO SIBARIS
9 HONKY TONK BLUES BAR
10 LA TERRRAZZA

SANTS-
MONTJUÏC

PASSATGE
DE TUBELLA

CARRER DE BERLIN

Jardins
d'Elisard
Sala

Abba Sants
Hotel

Jardins
de
Màlaga

L3

CARRER D'ENTENÇA

D'ARAGO

Hotel Catalonia
Roma

Hotel
Sercotel
Abbot

PLAÇA DEL
CENTRE

MELCIOR DE PALAU

L5

Sants
estació

L'EIXAMPLE

NOVA ESQUERRA
DE L'EIXAMPLE

CELLER DE
GELIDA

R1 R2 R2 Nord R2 Sud R3 R4

CARRER DE

TARRAGONA

Hotel
Sant
Angelo

ADDIS
ABEBA

Jardins de
Joaquim
Domingo i
Sanchez

Sants

CARRER DE BÉJAR

CARRER DE TARRAGONA

Parc de
Joan
Miró

SANTS

Parc de
l'Espanya
Industrial

CARRER DEL RECTOR TRIADÓ

L3

Hotel
Onix
Fira

TERRAVINO

LA
PARADETA

CARRER D'ENGARDA

Plaça
d'Herenni

Catalonia
Barcelona
Plaza

PLAÇA
DE
SANTS

HOMO
SIBARIS

HOSTAFRANCS

L1

CARRER DE

XOSTAFRANCS

SANTS

ESPANYA

MERCAT DE SANTS

LA TERE
GASTROBAR

Jardins de
Ramon Aramon
i Serra

CARRETERA DE LA BORDETA

HONKY TONK
BLUES BAR

CARRER DELS JOCS FLORALS

CARRER D'OLZINELLES

Ayre
Hotel
Gran Via

Jardins de
la Rambla
de Sants

Plaça
de la
Farga

Sala
Flyhard
Teatre

CARRER DEL MOIANÈS

GAVA

Hotel Azul
Barcelona

Hotel
Climent

N

TO
MARTINEZ
(SEE MAP LEFT) →

Caixaforum
Barcelona

CARRER

Jardins de
Celestina
Vigneaux
i Cibils

LA FONT
DE LA GUATLLA

FONT
MÀGICA
(MAGIC
FOUNTAIN)

BOMBONERIA
PONS

CARRER

R5 R50 R6 R60 S4 S8 S33 L8

BCN
Montjuïc

FRANCESC FERRER I GUARDIA

LA BORDETA

POBLE
ESPANYOL

LA
TERRRAZZA

RAMBLA DE BADAL

MAGÒRIA-
LA CAMPANA

GRAN VIA DE LES CORTS CATALANES

CARRER DE LA FONT FLORIDA

AVINGUDA DE

AVINGUDA DE L'ESTADI

0   50 m

Parc de la
Font
Florida

Parc de Montjuïc

Camp de Rugbi
de la
Foixarda

Piscines
Bernat
Picornell

Jardins del
Valent
Petit

LA MARINA
DE PORT

SANTS-
MONTJUÏC

Camp
Municipal de Futbol
Julià de Capmany

TORRE DE
COMUNICACIONS
DE MONTJUÏC
(SANTIAGO
CALATRAVA'S
OLYMPIC FLAME)

Parc de
Can
Sabaté

Golf
Montjuïc

1.

CELLER DE GELIDA

Carrer del Vallespir, 65
933 39 26 41
cellerdegelida.net
Open Mon–Fri 9am–2pm &
5–8.30pm, Sat 9.30am–2.30pm
Metro: Plaça del Centre

Located on tree-fringed Carrer de Vallespir (dangerously close to my apartment), this family-run bottle shop stocks more than 3500 wines from all over the world. Whether you'd like a bottle or two to enjoy in your hotel room or a few to squeeze in your suitcase, this place offers an excellent range. The family business dates back to 1895, but it boomed in the 1970s when Toni Falgueras, fourth-generation wine connoisseur, decided to go against the grain and focus on selling wines by the bottle instead of rustic wines by the gallon. Creaking wooden floorboards and a dungeon-like back room packed with rare vintages make it feel like you're shopping in the pantry of a medieval castle. With prices ranging from just 4€ up to 400€ a bottle, you can be sure to find something enticing. They offer discounts if you buy over a certain number of bottles.

BOMBONERIA PONS
Carrer Olzinelles, 78
933 32 70 46
bomboneriapons.com
Open Mon–Fri 8am–8pm,
Sat 9am–2pm
Metro: Mercat Nou

This artisanal chocolate factory and shop will take you back to the magic of your childhood. Dating to 1960, it is now run by the third generation of the Pons family. Each and every one of the creamy cocoa creations is handmade with love and beautifully packaged in gift boxes. The shop itself, with its luxurious wood panelling and elegant stained-glass windows, is like a luxury candy shop for grown-ups. The chocolates are displayed alongside giant handcrafted Easter eggs and chocolate sculptures of castles, teddy bears and monkeys – in fact, the giant chocolate monkeys are something of a local legend. They also make traditional turrón (nougat), which is less delicate than the chocolate and perfect for packing in your suitcase to take home as gifts.

ALMENDRA A LA FRAMBUESA

Almendra Marcona caramelizada, engordada en cobertura blanca y empolvada en polvo de frambuesa.

3.

LA TERE GASTROBAR

Carrer de Riego, 25
931 06 44 11
facebook.com/lateregastrobar
Open Tues–Sat 12–4pm (lunch)
& 7.30pm–12am (dinner), Sun
12–4pm (lunch) & 7.30–11pm
(dinner)
Metro: Plaça de Sants

One of the new breed of gastro-bars taking Sants by storm, La Tere is all about boutique Catalan wines and creative Spanish cuisine in a beautiful, modern space. The crisp white walls and minimalist decor look like something you'd find in a contemporary architecture magazine, but you can eat like royalty at La Tere even if you're on a budget. The low-lit bar area is great for pre-meal drinks and a few nibbles, while the deceptively large dining room out back is a stylish space to delve into Catalan chef José Viñals' fusion fare. Start with Spanish anchovies splashed in lime mayonnaise and wasabi, and tuna tatami with sesame and kimchi. Mains include octopus brochettes with paprika-peppered potato, sticky barbecue ribs, and lamb chops served with fresh yoghurt and mint. The three-course evening menu includes wine and a cocktail, a bargain at 35€.

MARTINEZ

Carretera de Miramar, 38
931 06 60 52
martinezbarcelona.com
Open Mon–Sun 1pm–1am
Metro: Espanya

Perched atop one of Montjuïc's cactus-clad cliffs, this secluded restaurant and bar offers breathtaking views over the Mediterranean Sea. It's hidden well off the tourist trail and takes a little bit of legwork to get to (or a scenic taxi ride), which is probably why so many locals head here to escape the summer crowds. Order a jug of cava sangria and sit out on the sun terrace to soak up some rays. Try as you might, it's almost impossible to resist the aromas of freshly grilled lobster and prawns with garlic and lemon - the paella is excellent too. Martinez is best at sunset, when the colourful string lights glow against the candy-floss sky.

5.

TERRAVINO

Carrer de Santa Caterina, 6
677 24 59 66
facebook.com/pages/Terravino-BCN/1134954183201886
Open Tues–Thurs 11am–4pm (lunch) & 7pm–12am (dinner), Fri 11am–4pm (lunch) & 7pm–2am (dinner), Sat 12–4pm (lunch) & 8pm–2am (dinner), Sun 8pm–12am (dinner)
Metro: Plaça de Sants

This little wine bar behind a plum-hued facade is a great place to sup quality Catalan wines without blowing your budget. It's the creation of two wine lovers, Isabel Garcia and Cecilia Osorio, who display their latest discoveries on the wall as if they were works of art. They stock a broad selection of wines from across Spain, but the variety from Catalonia's world-class vineyards are particularly delightful. Ask for recommendations and enjoy a relaxed afternoon – if you're lucky, you might catch one of their live music performances. Pair your wine with top-quality Iberian ham, gourmet olives and a selection of Spanish cheeses for the ultimate taste of Spain. The 18€ wine-tasting menu with tapas is an absolute bargain.

6.

LA PARADETA

Carrer de Riego, 27
934 31 90 59
laparadeta.com
Open Tues–Thurs 1–4pm (lunch) & 8–11.30pm (dinner), Fri–Sat 1–4pm (lunch) & 8pm–12am (dinner), Sun 1–4pm
Metro: Plaça de Sants

Eating fish and shellfish is a must in Barcelona, but it's all too easy to find yourself paying inflated tourist prices for low-quality food. The team at La Paradeta keep quality high and prices low with their unique system: you point out what you'd like at the fishmonger-style counter (paradeta translates to 'market stall') and receive a ticket; a cook grabs your selection straight off the ice, and they call you when it's ready. Whether it's crab, prawns, mussels or lobster, the result is an astonishingly delicious and affordable way to eat market-fresh seafood. Pair it with one of the famous white wines from the north of Spain for a truly satisfying fish feast. There are four branches around the city, but the one in Sants is the original and still considered the best.

LOCAL TIP

Check out the nearby Modernist Mercat de Sants (Carrer de Sant Jordi, 6), which hums along to the groove of laid-back local life and is surrounded by little cafes and cute bodegas (wine bars).

7.

ADDIS ABEBA

Carrer del Vallespir, 44
934 09 40 37
addis-abeba.es
Open Tues–Fri 8pm–12am,
Sat–Sun 1.30–4pm (lunch) &
8pm–12am (dinner)
Metro: Plaça del Centre

This family-run restaurant offers authentic Ethiopian cuisine in an alluringly warm and exotic space. African masks, pottery and musical instruments bring the exposed walls to life, while spellbinding Ethiopian beats transport you to a faraway land. Diners huddle around rainbow-coloured mesobs (woven wicker tables) on wooden stools and dig into delicious sharing plates. Dishes like the vegetarian-friendly pumpkin stew with leek and fragrant spices, and the house special dorowot chicken stew, are served in traditional earthenware dishes. You eat with your hands, using injera (a sort of spongy flatbread) to scoop up the food. Be sure to ask about the selection of Ethiopian beers, which complement the food beautifully. The 17.50€ set menu is an excellent way to try a selection of different dishes, and includes a drink and dessert.

HOMO SIBARIS

Plaça d'Osca, 4
931 85 66 93
homosibaris.com
Open Mon–Thurs 5.30pm–
12am, Fri 5.30pm–2am,
Sat 1pm–2am, Sun 1pm–12am
Metro: Plaça de Sants

This craft beer bar, opened in
2011, was one of Barcelona's
first, helping to kickstart
Barcelona's brewing
revolution. Owner Guillem
Laporta is something of a
local hero and champions
quality brews from local
artisans. His main focus is
on unfiltered, unpasteurised
beer, which means the taps
pump out some of the freshest
and most interesting beers
in town. The chalk-scrawled
blackboards behind the bar
display whatever's currently
on draught, and there are
countless bottled options to
choose from. If you're feeling
overwhelmed, ask Guillem for
a couple of tasters –he can
often be found sipping away
at a pint and chatting about
his latest finds. He speaks
excellent English, so don't
be shy. Make sure to check
out Homo Sibaris' bottle shop
too, where you can pick up
all sorts of rare brews from
local artisans.

LOCAL TIP
Not far from here is the
lively Parc de l'Espanya
Industrial, where you
can relax by a lake and
watch the locals practising
their dance moves or
playing basketball.

HONKY TONK BLUES BAR

Carrer de Finlàndia, 45
934 22 95 98
facebook.com/
honkytonk.bluesbar
Open Wed–Thurs 7.30pm–
2am, Fri–Sat 7.30pm–3am,
Sun 7.30pm–2am
Metro: Plaça de Sants

Barcelona is celebrated as the cradle of Spanish blues music, and this intimate venue is where the best local and international artists perform. The wood-clad walls and bourbon-drenched bar give it the feel of a classic New Orleans dive bar, while the rockabilly regulars add to the vibe with their high-octane outfits. Shows start at 8.30pm on Saturdays and Sundays, with everything from solo acoustic sets to larger groups featuring honky tonk piano, double bass, silky slide guitar and trainwreck harmonica. Sip a Jack and Coke or one of the many imported American craft beers and rock the night away in one of the rickety old chairs. Entry is free, so you'll want to get there as early as possible to secure one of the front-row tables.

10.

LA TERRRAZZA

Avenida Francesc Ferrer I
Guardia
687 96 98 25
laterrrazza.com
Open Thurs–Sat 2pm–6am
Metro: Espanya

Tucked away in the courtyard of a mansion in Poble Espanyol (an imitation village celebrating the architecture of Spain), this haven of hedonism is the place to go for electronic house music and outdoor partying. The club has space for around 1000 people, which lends it an intimate air of exclusivity, while the bartenders are legendary for their colourful cocktail concoctions.

Swaying palm trees cast dancing shadows and renowned DJs like James Priestley, Ricardo Villalobos and Larry Heard keep the beats grinding until sunrise. It's fun and unrestrained, with the vibe of an Ibiza beach party. The backstage VIP areas are the perfect place to celebrate with friends on your own private dance floor. You'll get discounted entry (5€ instead of 10€) if you go before 2am.

Located just a few footsteps away from the main transport hub of Sants Station, **Parc de l'Espanya Industrial** is built on the site of an old textile mill. Stroll around its huge lake and explore the basketball courts and ping-pong tables before stretching out on the grass to enjoy a siesta. Not bad for a park plonked right next to a busy train station!

From Plaça Espanya you can walk up to Montjuïc, where your first port of call should be the magnificent **Museu Nacional d'Art de Catalunya (MNAC)** (Carrer de Verdi, 32, cines-verdi.com/barcelona). Housed in the Neo-Baroque Palau Nacional (National Palace), it's a romantic and exuberant place to explore the many Romanesque frescoes and Catalan Gothic paintings inside. The views from the cafe terrace out front will stay with you forever. Hang around until dusk to witness the famous 'Magic Fountain' music, water and light show.

Just behind MNAC is the fascinating **Museu Olímpic** (Avinguda de l'Estadi, 60, museuolimpicbcn.cat) and the **Jardí Botànic** (Carrer Doctor i Font Quer, museuciencies. cat/es/visitanos/jardi-botanic), a botanic garden home to more than 1000 species. Don't miss the **Estadi Olímpic Lluís Companys** (Passeig Olímpic, 15–17, estadiolimpic.cat), the Olympic stadium where you will find the iconic Montjuïc Communications Tower.

Martin Ebner is owner and personal trainer at Ebylife (Ebylife.com), a premier health and fitness company for residents and visitors in Barcelona.

Cementiri Montjuïc
(Carrer de la Mare de Déu de Port, 56–58): Dramatically located on one of the rocky slopes of Montjuïc hill, this cemetery is home to more than a million burials and has a mix of classic, Gothic and Art Nouveau styles. The views are incredible and you won't get the crowds of tourists you see at many other city spots.

Castell de Montjuïc
(Carretera de Montjuïc, 66): Sitting 173 metres (568 feet) above the port, Montjuïc Castle offers spectacular 360-degree views of the city. During the summer months, the castle hosts a fab outdoor cinema!

Piscina Municipal de Montjuïc
(Avinguda Miramar, 31): Talk about a pool with a view! This fancy Olympic swimming pool was designed by Antoni de Moragas for the 1992 Olympic diving events. It's well worth a visit in July and August, when it's open to the public.

Parc de Montjuïc
Montjuïc Park is my go-to for outdoor exercise – a beautiful green escape from the hustle and bustle of Barcelona city. Right beside the spiky Montjuïc Communications Tower you'll find a lovely terraced park, which is ideal for a picnic with friends.

Poble Espanyol
(Avinguda Francesc Ferrer I Guardia, 13): This open-air architectural museum is about 400 metres (1312 feet) away from the Fountains of Montjuïc. I love the flamenco performances on Saturdays; you feel as if you've been transported back in time.

Resting at the foot of Montjuïc, this once-quiet neighbourhood is now one of Barcelona's best places to eat, drink and party, made all the more charming by its laid-back pace of life. Literally translated, Poble Sec means 'Dry Village', but its lively nightlife ensures it's anything but.

Carrer Blai is the neighbourhood's main gastronomic vein, a half-kilometre-long pedestrianised street lined with wallet-friendly tapas bars. Day and night, this hedonistic playground throngs with foodies who are drawn by the bargain pintxos (a type of tapas from the Basque Country in northern Spain). With 'pintxo and drink for 2€' deals almost everywhere, the order of the day is to hop from bar to bar, nibbling, sipping and making new friends.

POBLE ЅEC

24   JUN 8016

ЅHOP
1   Brummell Ѕouvenir Ѕhop

EAT AND DRINK
2   Ѕpice Café
3   Blai 9
4   Mano Rota
5   The Tatami Room
6   Plaça Del Sortidor
7   Malamén

17

DRINK
8   Tinta Roja
9   El Molina
10 La Confitería

N

Hotel
Millenni

Teatre
Tantarantana

CARRER DE LES FLORS

Jardins de
Sant Pau
del Camp

CARRER D'ALDANA

RONDA DE SANT PAU

L2

LA CONFITERÍA

EL RAVAL

SANT PAU

CARRER DE LES TAPIES

CARRER

**SANT
ANTONI**

CARRER DE

Hotel
Barcelona
Universal

Auto
Hogar
Hotel

Barts
Teatre

PARAL·LEL

AVINGUDA   DEL   PARAL·LEL

L3

AVINGUDA   DEL   PARAL·LEL

Tryp
Apolo
Hotel

Teatre
Apolo

Teatre
Condal

Hotel
Paral·lel

EL MOLINO

Teatre
Victòria

CARRER DE POETA CABANYES

**THE
TATAMI
ROOM**

CARRER DE VILA I VILÀ

SALVÀ

EL POBLE SEC

CARRER DEL ROSER

HIROSHIMA

Funicular de Montjuïc

CARRER NOU DE LA RAMBLA

TO
MANO ROTA,
TINTA ROJA
SPICE CAFE,
MALAMÉN AND
PLAÇA DEL SORTIDOR
(SEE MAP LEFT)

CARRER DE PIQUER

CARRER D'EN FONTRODONA

CARRER DEL

Hotel
Coronado

CARRER

BLAI 9

CARRER DE BLAI

CARRER DE

Hotel
Nuevo
Triunfo

CARRER DE LAFONT

CARRER DE PIQUER

CARRER DE CABANES

CARRER DEN
FONTRODONA

CARRER DE

BLESA

**SANTS-
MONTJUÏC**

SALVA

**BRUMMELL
SOUVENIR
SHOP**

ROSER

**THE
GARAGE**

CARRER DE
MAGALHAES

PASSEIG DE   MONTJUÏC

Parc del
Mirador del
Poble Sec

REFUGI
307

CARRER DEL

CARRER

CARRER NOU DE LA RAMBLA

Parc
de la
Primavera

CAMÍ   DE   LA   FONT   TROBADA

Parc de Montjuïc

PASSEIG   DE   MIRAMAR

PASSEIG   DE   MIRAMAR

AVINGUDA   DE   MIRAMAR

0   50 m

PISCINA
MUNICIPAL
DE MONTJUÏC

CARRETERA   DE   MONTJUÏC

183

1.

BRUMMELL SOUVENIR SHOP

Nou de la Rambla, 174
Hotel Brummell lobby
931 25 86 22
hotelbrummell.com
Open Mon–Sun 24hrs
Metro: Poble Sec

Tucked away in the lobby of the boutique Hotel Brummell, this sanctuary of style and design is a great place to pick up atypical souvenirs. Part shop, part studio, the idea is to curate uncommon items ranging from handprinted stationery and illustrations to Barcelona-themed reading material and retro Polaroid cameras. You'll also find a selection of fashion-forward clothing and accessories, from swimwear and sunglasses to sunhats and beach bags. Each piece has been carefully selected by chief curator Talissa Lollu, who will happily reveal their backstories. The hotel also has a range of fold-up Brompton bikes and electric bikes for rent, which are perfect for exploring the nearby mountain of Montjuïc.

2

SPICE CAFÉ

Carrer de Margarit, 13
936 24 33 59
spicecafe.es
Open Tues–Thurs 4–9pm,
Fri–Sat 11am–9pm
Metro: Poble Sec

This cosy little cafe is where Barcelona's coffee and cake lovers go when they're in need of a serious fix. Everything from the chunky choc-chip cookies and muffins to the cakes and brownies are baked to perfection in-house and served in prodigious proportions. Flavours change daily, but you can expect the likes of ricotta and cinnamon cheesecake, coconut cake with pistachio and lime, and a mean apple pie. The cake that cemented Spice's now-legendary reputation is the double-tiered carrot cake. Spiked with cinnamon, nutmeg, vanilla and cloves, and lavished with a rich cream cheese frosting, it really is the perfect mid-afternoon merienda (snack). Pair with the excellent coffee made with beans from local roasters Café de Finca. There's also a selection of beer from Barcelona's iconic Moritz brewery. On weekends, they also serve bagels with a variety of tempting fillings .

3.

BLAI 9

Carrer de Blai, 9
933 29 73 65
blai9.com
Open Sun–Thurs 9–12am,
Fri–Sat 9–1am
Metro: Paral·lel

Carrer Blai's famous pintxo (tapas) bars may all be cheap and cheerful, but not all of them are known for creativity. At Blai 9, owners Oscar Sala and Simone Ortega have done away with the rulebook and created what have to be the most interesting flavour combinations in the neighbourhood. Huge platters line the bar, where you can choose toothpick-spiked bites like chorizo and potato pancakes with poached quail eggs, and mini Angus burgers with havarti cheese, caramelised onions and mustard. Prices start at just 2€ for a drink (the vermouth's great) and a pintxo, making it an affordable place to spend an afternoon exploring new flavours. The international crowd makes it a fun place to hang out at any time of day. The different-coloured toothpicks denote various prices – check out the blackboards to see the price of each colour before piling up your plate.

4.

MANO ROTA

Carrer de la Creu dels Molers, 4
931 64 80 41
manorota.com
Open Mon–Wed 8–11.30pm,
Thurs–Sat 1–3.30pm (lunch)
& 8–11.30pm (dinner),
Sun 1–3.30pm
Metro: Poble Sec

Chefs Bernat Bermudo and Oswaldo Brito elevate Catalan market cuisine with international ingredients and their own style of non-conformist cooking. The focus is very much on showcasing quality seasonal produce, but the pair isn't afraid to show off what they learned as young chefs abroad. This global mindset really shines in dishes like aguachile de mejillones: mussels drizzled in a light and zesty Chilean salsa of lime, coriander and chilli peppers, while those like the marmitako (tuna stew with avocado) show a deep respect for Spain's classic cookbook. The friendly service, white walls and exposed brickwork provide a casual ambience – no need to get glammed up, though no one will flinch if you do. Treat yourself to the 11-course tasting menu (60€ – great value considering the quality). Dishes change daily depending on whatever's freshest at the market; there is no printed copy of the menu.

5.

THE TATAMI ROOM

Carrer del Poeta Cabanyes, 19
933 29 67 40
thetatamiroombcn.com
Open Tues–Thurs 1.30–
3.30pm (lunch) & 8–11.30pm
(dinner), Fri 1.30–3.30pm
(lunch) & 8pm–12am (dinner),
Sat 1.30–3.30pm (lunch) &
8pm–12am (dinner)
Metro: Paral·lel

Serving authentic Japanese
tempura, nigiri, sashimi and
ramen, The Tatami Room is
a paradise for Japanophiles.
British owner Hugo Lonsdale
honed his noodle- and sushi-
making skills in Tokyo before
moving to Barcelona with
his Japanese wife. Cherry
blossom-bedecked lamp
shades and colourful works
of art combine to create a
cocoon of tranquillity. Diners
sit on tatami mats and eat at
traditional floor-level tables,
but not before being invited
to remove their shoes. Order
a selection of lightly seared
tuna and salmon nigiri
drizzled with chef Nao's
secret sauce, and salmon
maki tempura with sweet
teriyaki, chives and sesame
seeds. The miso ramen (pork
and chicken broth with
miso) is just €8.50 – a great
way to eat well on a budget.
There are also excellent
vegan options, such as
the Tan Tan black sesame
ramen. Enjoy with a cold
Asahi beer or a sake for the
full experience.

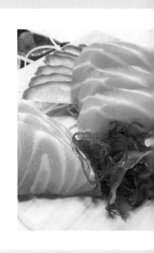

6.

PLAÇA DEL SORTIDOR

Poble Sec has become a mecca for foodies, which means it can get a bit crowded at times, but you won't have to concern yourself about the hordes if you head to secluded Plaça del Sortidor. Lined with a great selection of tapas bars and restaurants and filled with tree-shaded terraces, it's an ideal spot for a lazy lunch in the sun.

The main attraction is the ancient **El Sortidor de la Filomena Pagès**, a colourful Modernist tapas bar dating back to 1908. It has retained its bohemian charm with beautiful stained-glass windows, hefty marble tables and old wooden chairs, it's a vibrant space to explore traditional Catalan vermouth and tapas. Just next door, **Luki** is a small, artsy restaurant offering creative Mediterranean dishes and local wines. The weekday menu del día (set lunch menu, 10.90€) offers unbeatable value for money. On the other side of the square, **El Carro Gros** has a sunny outdoor terrace that is a good spot for a couple of casual drinks and nibbles.

7.

MALAMÉN

Carrer de Blai, 53
932 52 77 63
malamen.es
Open Tues–Sun 8pm–12am
Metro: Poble Sec

This high-end restaurant is one of the hippest, most delicious places to eat on Carrer Blai. The space itself is fairly tiny, but the decadent decor is bold and full of personality: think black-on-gold leather stools, angular mirrors that span an entire wall and crackling Edison bulbs that come together to create a sort of hipsterfied Art Deco look. Italian chef Alessio Menna creatively fuses elements of his native cuisine with classic Spanish flavours, changing the menu with each season. Try dishes like beetroot tartare with miso mustard and salads like berries with edible flowers drizzled in a zingy Catalan cava vinaigrette. Or go full Mediterranean with fresh fish, grilled meats and seasonal vegetables. There's a particularly excellent wine menu, and the staff seem to get a kick out of revealing their latest finds. With its reasonable prices, Malamén is a great choice for those who want a fine dining experience without breaking the bank.

8.

TINTA ROJA

Carrer de la Creu dels
Molers, 17
934 43 32 43
tintaroja.cat
Open Wed 8.30pm–1am,
Thurs 8.30pm–2am, Fri–Sat
8.30pm–3am
Metro: Poble Sec

Hidden on a quiet side street in the heart of Poble Sec, this Argentinian cocktail bar and clandestine theatre will bring out your Latino fire. As you enter, you'll be greeted by the sounds of gentle jazz and bartenders shaking up colourful concoctions in vintage tumblers. But the magic doesn't reveal itself until you walk through the narrow corridors, which are dimly lit by flickering gas lamps and filled with antique sofas and pictures of famous tango dancers from bygone eras. Pull back the red velvet curtain to discover the secret performance space with circus trapeze ropes that tumble from the ceiling and full of the ethereal twinkle of fairy lights. It holds regular music performances, acting classes and their legendary milongas (tango events, on the first and third Wednesday of every month). The house special caña legui cocktail, made with a punchy sugarcane liquor, lemon juice, orange and cinnamon, will get you dancing in no time.

9.

EL MOLINO

Carrer de Vila i Vilà, 99
932 05 51 11
elmolinobcn.com
Opening times vary
Metro: Paral·lel

This 19th-century theatre
is Barcelona's equivalent
of London's West End and
New York's Broadway. The
illuminated spinning windmill
out the front was inspired by
Paris' Moulin Rouge cabaret
hall, hinting at the electrifying
shows this venue is famous
for. The ritzy rooftop 'Golden
Bar' is a fancy place to sip
premium-grade cocktails and
Spanish wines, with live piano
and views over the bustling
street life below. The live
music performances offer a
chance to see flamenco, jazz,
blues and Catalan rumba.
Sit close to the stage, but
only if you're feeling daring:
you may well be pulled out
of your seat to join in with
the performers.

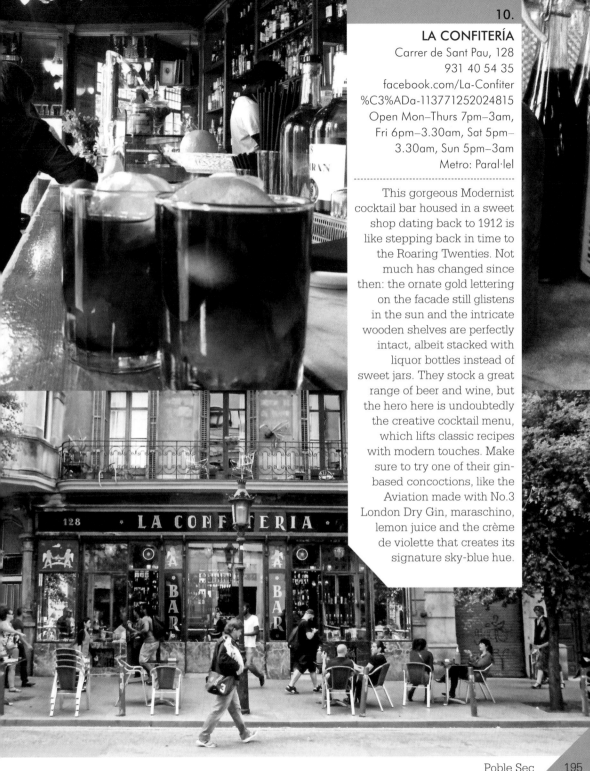

10

LA CONFITERÍA

Carrer de Sant Pau, 128
931 40 54 35
facebook.com/La-Confiter
%C3%ADa-113771252024815
Open Mon–Thurs 7pm–3am,
Fri 6pm–3.30am, Sat 5pm–
3.30am, Sun 5pm–3am
Metro: Paral·lel

This gorgeous Modernist cocktail bar housed in a sweet shop dating back to 1912 is like stepping back in time to the Roaring Twenties. Not much has changed since then: the ornate gold lettering on the facade still glistens in the sun and the intricate wooden shelves are perfectly intact, albeit stacked with liquor bottles instead of sweet jars. They stock a great range of beer and wine, but the hero here is undoubtedly the creative cocktail menu, which lifts classic recipes with modern touches. Make sure to try one of their gin-based concoctions, like the Aviation made with No.3 London Dry Gin, maraschino, lemon juice and the crème de violette that creates its signature sky-blue hue.

Visit **Hiroshima** (Vila i Vilà
61–67, hiroshima.cat) for mind-
expanding performance art,
ranging from experimental live
music to contemporary circus
and dance. For something
considerably less mentally
taxing, take a stroll up to the
verdant **Parc del Mirador
del Poble Sec** (Passeig de
Montjuïc, 28) for tranquillity
and spectacular views
across Barcelona.

Experience how many of
Barcelona's residents lived
during the Spanish Civil War
at the sobering **Refugi 307**
(Carrer Nou de la Rambla,
175, ajuntament.barcelona.
cat/museuhistoria/en/muhba-
refugi-307). This fascinating air-
raid shelter was built in 1937 by
the locals to protect themselves
against dictator General
Franco's bombings. Tours are
available on Sundays and held
in English at 10.30am – be
sure to reserve your place
in advance.

Seek out the beautiful
Parròquia Santa Madrona
(Carrer de Tapioles, 10), an
impressive Neo-Gothic church
tucked away on an unassuming
residential street. Built between
1884 and 1888, it is dedicated
to Saint Madrona, who
Barcelonians once worshipped
as a defender against illness,
protector of sailors and bringer
of rain. Though the saint is
largely forgotten, annual
festivities are held to celebrate
her on March 5.

Andre Arriaza runs Barcelona Eat Local Food Tours (barcelonaeatlocal. com), which provides culinary and cultural experiences in Barcelona's most fascinating neighbourhoods.

Jardins de les Tres Xemeneies (Avinguda del Parallel, 49): I love the eclectic ambience and the mix of graffiti and skateboarding at the 'three chimneys garden'. The three chimneys here, which used to serve the Barcelona Traction, Light and Power Company Ltd, represent the city's industrial past.

Yoga at the Garage by Veronica Blume (Carrer de Magalhães): Yoga here reminds me of my old stomping grounds in Brooklyn, New York; the vintage space is lovely and the location, an old garage that forms part of Hotel Brummell, is close to the entrance of the excellent park Mirador de Poble Sec.

El Catascopio (Carrer de Margarit, 17): I love that you can buy the work of the artists who show their work here and actually talk to them, as well. The staff are really nice and knowledgeable.

Celler Cal Marino (Carrer de Margarit, 54): This is one of my favourite wine shops in town, especially because of their organic wine selection and tapas. Don't let its darkness and old-school ambience deter you!

La Tomaquera (Carrer de Margarit): This is my choice when I am in need of local countryside cuisine. I love the snails in tomato sauce and lamb chops. Pretty informal and down to earth, this place makes you feel that you are truly in Catalonia.

SANT ANTONI

BODEGA 1900

CARRER DE TAMARIT

CARRER D'ENTENÇA

TO
MAP RIGHT
(VIA AVINGUDA
DEL PARAL·LEL)

AVINGUDA DEL PARAL·LEL ➡

L3

AVINGUDA DEL PARAL·LEL

EL
POBLE
SEC

ʃANT ANTONI

Despite its central location, this tree-fringed, quiet enclave was little more than a sleepy residential area until recently. But as locals and tourists discovered its friendly atmosphere and casual bodegas (wine bars), it morphed into one of Barcelona's hippest neighbourhoods. There's always something happening here, albeit in its own laid-back way.

With its russet-red ironwork and ornate Modernist detailing, Mercat de Sant Antoni has always been the historic heart of the neighbourhood. But as the area lures increasingly cool crowds, its cultural centre is shifting to nearby Carrer del Parlament, a sprawling street where boutiques, brunch spots, tapas bars and bodegas seem to open on a weekly basis.

24   JUN 8976

ʃHOP
1 TRAIT ʃTORE
2 EL RECIBIDOR
ʃHOP AND DRINK
3 HORCHATERIA ʃIRVENT
EAT
4 LA DONUTERIA
5 THE JUICE HOUSE

17

EAT AND DRINK
6 JOVANI & VINS
7 TARANNÀ CAFÈ
8 BARNA BREW
9 ELS ʃORTIDORS
10 BODEGA 1900

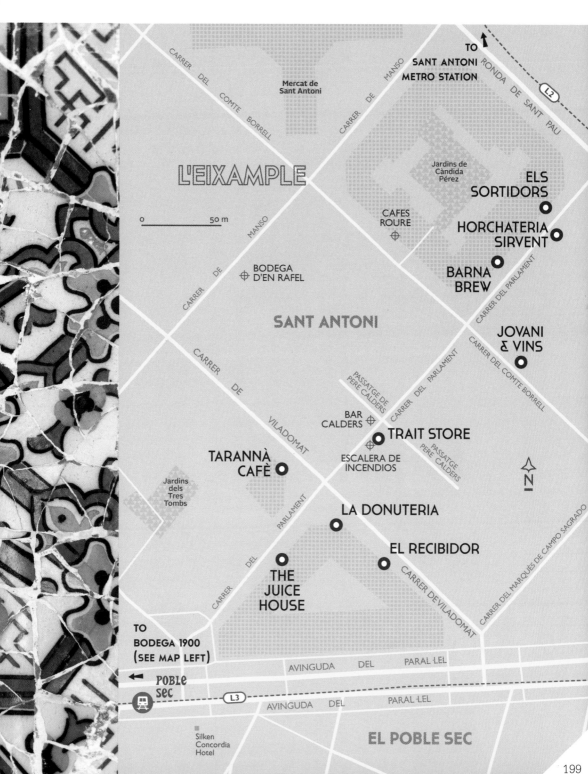

CARRER DEL COMTE BORRELL

Mercat de
Sant Antoni

CARRER DE MANSO

TO
**SANT ANTONI
METRO STATION**

RONDA DE SANT PAU

L2

L'EIXAMPLE

Jardins de
Càndida
Pérez

**ELS
SORTIDORS**

CARRER DE MANSO

CAFES
ROURE

**HORCHATERIA
SIRVENT**

0   50 m

CARRER DE

**BODEGA
D'EN RAFEL**

**BARNA
BREW**

CARRER DEL PARLAMENT

SANT ANTONI

**JOVANI
& VINS**

CARRER DEL COMTE BORRELL

CARRER DE

PASSATGE DE
PERE CALDERS

CARRER DEL PARLAMENT

VILADOMAT

BAR
CALDERS

TRAIT STORE

PASSATGE DE
PERE CALDERS

**TARANNÀ
CAFÈ**

ESCALERA DE
INCENDIOS

Jardins
dels
Tres
Tombs

N

LA DONUTERIA

PARLAMENT

EL RECIBIDOR

CARRER DEL MARQUES DE CAMPO SAGRADO

CARRER DE VILADOMAT

**THE
JUICE
HOUSE**

CARRER DEL

TO
BODEGA 1900
(SEE MAP LEFT)

AVINGUDA   DEL   PARAL·LEL

**POBLE
SEC**

L3

AVINGUDA   DEL   PARAL·LEL

Silken
Concordia
Hotel

EL POBLE SEC

1.

TRAIT STORE

Carrer del Parlament, 28
936 67 16 31
traitstore.com
Open Mon–Sat 11am–2pm &
4–8.30pm
Metro: Poble Sec

A union between fashionistas
Gabriel Ortiz and João
Novaes, Trait Store is an
independent boutique run
'by hipsters, for hipsters'.
The pseudo-cinema billboard
sign out front hints at the
contemporary decor within,
which is all wood-on-white,
unpolished concrete walls
and prickly cactus plants. It's
neat and pristine, featuring
a cherry-picked selection
of fashion-forward clothing
and perfectly displayed
accessories. Find the latest
looks, from knitwear, jeans
and jackets to shorts,
shirts and T-shirts. Brands
include the likes of Rita
Row from the nearby Costa
Brava and Korean-London
brand Side Party, as well
as Barcelona-based brands
like Laser, Verdugo and
Oldend. Shoe lovers will
adore the retro range of Vans
and Converse alongside
contemporary kicks from
Reebok and Adidas.

2.

EL RECIBIDOR

Carrer de Viladomat, 9
935 30 42 21
elrecibidor.com
Open Mon–Fri 4–8pm,
Sat 11am–2pm & 4–8pm
Metro: Poble Sec

This vintage furniture boutique celebrates the subtle elegance of the '50s, '60s and '70s. It's the creation of Gerard Thomas and Antonio Dos Santo (both ex-advertising art directors), and Jorge Carrascosa (an ex-filmmaker), who came together through their shared passion for mid-century Modernist design. Pieces range from restored teak coffee tables shipped in from Norway and England to newly crafted ceramics from Denmark and Germany that harken to design epochs gone by. There are plenty of walnut-wood armchairs and minimalist Nordic sofas that look like they've come straight off the set of *Madmen*. Retro wooden toys and vintage maps and posters – like the 1960s cycling circus bear poster from the Soviet Union and the 1980s Moscow Olympics sailing poster – will fit nicely into your luggage. They also offer a first-rate shipping service.

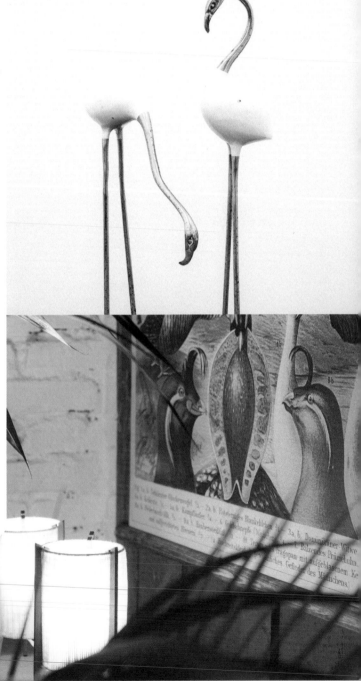

HORCHATERIA SIRVENT

Carrer del Parlament, 56
934 41 27 20
turronessirvent.com
Open Mon–Sun 9am–10pm
Metro: Sant Antoni

Spain's traditional turrón (nougat) is the perfect treat when you're craving something sweet, and Horchateria Sirvent is where the locals go for the best of the best. Dating back to 1920, this family-run business is one of the oldest horchaterias in Barcelona and crafts artisanal slabs of turrón with toasted almonds, honey, sugar and egg whites. Modern recipes also include ingredients like praline, candied fruit, coconut, chocolate and even boozy liquors. They also make their own range of artisanal ice-cream. Retro sundaes, served in giant glass tulip dishes with all the trimmings, and refreshing milkshakes hit the spot on a hot summer's day. Don't miss the traditional Spanish horchata, which is similar to a milkshake but made with ground tiger nuts instead of ice-cream.

4.

LA DONUTERIA

Carrer del Parlament, 20
933 29 75 11
ladonuteria.com
Open Mon–Fri 8am–8pm,
Sat–Sun 9am–9pm
Metro: Poble Sec

You've never seen such beautiful doughnuts, handmade in an open-fronted kitchen by American pastry chef Richard Bies. These artisanal brioche beauties are made with the highest quality ingredients and cooked in small batches, so they're always fresh. Flavours change on a daily basis, but you can expect colourful combinations like banana and coffee with cocoa nibs, bacon with maple syrup and apple, and apricot with pistachio. If you can't make up your mind, then go for Richard's classic Tahitian vanilla-bean glaze. They also serve quality coffee in generous takeaway cups, which are perfect for dunking your dough.

5.

THE JUICE HOUSE
Carrer del Parlament, 12
931 17 15 15
thejuicehouse.es
Open Mon–Thurs 11am–4pm
& 7–11pm, Fri–Sat 10–12am,
Sun 10am–9pm
Metro: Poble Sec

The Juice House is one of
few places in Barcelona
dedicated to clean eating.
The creation of Daniela
Luzzatto and Luz Cortázar,
two friends from Venezuela,
the dining space is warm and
inviting, with wooden crates
full of fruit stacked up by the
juice bar and huge murals
painted on the walls. Fuel
your body with a Super Food
Bowl that includes roasted
chickpeas with turmeric,
quinoa, red cabbage with
cinnamon and wasabi tahini.
Sip cold-pressed juices
like the Hardcore Green
with kale, spinach, fennel,
apple, pineapple and ginger.
Creative homemade cakes,
such as lime and avocado
tart with dates, nuts and
chocolate, are proof that
healthy can also be decadent.
The prices here are tasty too;
you can eat seriously well for
15 to 20€. Skip the brunch
rush and visit later in the day
for chilled-out vibes.

6.

JOVANI & VINS

Carrer del Comte Borrell, 30
935 39 40 02
jovanivins.com
Open Tues–Sat 10am–2pm &
5–10pm
Metro: Poble Sec

If you're keen to explore the wines of Catalonia, then this family-run wine shop and tasting space is just the place. Siblings Montsa, Sergi and Roberto Jovani were fortunate enough to inherit a vineyard in the nearby Penedès wine region, where they produce their award-winning Berdié cava. They opened Jovani & Vins because they wanted somewhere in Barcelona to connect with their customers and celebrate the many world-class wines of the region. The shelves are stacked with more than 300 wines from local vineyards, with bottles starting at less than 10€ a pop. You can also pick up a selection of gourmet Catalan cheeses and cured meats to take home with you. Out the back, there's a cosy tasting space where the sommeliers hold weekly tastings. The cheese and wine pairing sessions are unmissable.

LOCAL TIP
If Jovani & Vins puts you in the mood for more wine, pull up a chair on the sunny terrace at Bar Calders (Carrer del Parlament, 25) around the corner.

7.

TARANNÀ CAFÈ

Carrer de Viladomat, 23
931 06 11 93
tarannacafe.com
Open Mon 9am–5pm, Tues–
Fri 9–1am, Sat 9.30–1.30am,
Sun 10am–5pm
Metro: Poble Sec

This cool corner cafe
epitomises what makes
Sant Antoni so hip. Its
bottle-green facade opens
up with huge windows,
connecting the interior with
the street and its flower-
potted terrace. It's the kind of
place where you could easily
while away an afternoon
with coffee and a good
book. The menu changes
with the seasons and all
produce is sourced from the
famous La Boqueria market
(see p. 039) on La Rambla.
Indulge in beautifully
cooked quiches served with
crunchy asparagus, gourmet
sandwiches and fresh fish
with grilled vegetables.

Hearty brunch options like
the ous al forn (oven-baked
eggs) make for a beautiful
way to start the day, as do
the homemade cakes. Try
a wedge of the Guinness
cake with chocolate and
mascarpone, or the dreamy
red velvet cake.

8.

BARNA BREW

Carrer del Parlament, 45
674 41 56 18
facebook.com/BarnaBrew
Open Tues–Thurs 5.30–
11.30pm, Fri 5.30pm–1.30am,
Sat 12pm–1.30am,
Sun 12–11.30pm
Metro: Sant Antoni

With a huge onsite brewery
and a menu packed with
creative tapas dishes, this
vibrant brewpub is a great
spot for sipping craft beer
on Sant Antoni's trendy
Carrer del Parlament. The
earthy, unpolished walls and
vintage furnishings lend
the space a sort of romantic
French feel that nods to the
bar's fascinating backstory.
Years ago, owner Alex
Lazarowicz moved from his
native London to embark on
a political career in Brussels.
It didn't take long for him
to fall in love with Belgian
beer and, more importantly,
a girl from Barcelona. With
dreams of starting their
lives together in the Catalan
capital, Alex and Carlota quit
their jobs and moved. That's
how Alex ended up building
the brewery and bar where
he crafts his award-winning
range of Belgian-inspired
Catalan beers. Start with
the light and crispy Pils
Parlament before moving
on to the blonde ale, dark
ale and IPA. The food is
great too – try the Moreneta
veal burger.

LOCAL TIP
Check out Sant Antoni's popular flea market, which takes over Carrer del Comte d'Urgell from 8.30am to 2.30pm every Sunday.

9.

ELS SORTIDORS

Carrer del Parlament, 53
934 41 16 02
elssortidors.com
Open Mon–Thurs 5pm–12am,
Fri–Sun 12pm–12am
Metro: Sant Antoni

This stylish-but-homey bodega (wine bar) and tapas restaurant buzzes day and night with locals enjoying its staggering selection. Housed in an old motorcycle mechanic's workshop, the cavernous space is packed to the rafters with wine barrels full of local vino and vermouth, which you can buy by the glass at eye-poppingly low prices. Head deeper into the cosy space and you'll find shelves stacked with wines and craft beers from every corner of Spain. Do as the locals do and pull up at one of the old wine barrel tables to indulge in gourmet Spanish cheeses, cold cuts and olives, making the afternoon stretch out into evening. Don't miss the excellent ensaladia rusa (Russian salad), which, belying its name, is a classic Spanish potato salad with carrots, peas, apples, celery, onion and mayo.

LOCAL TIP
Just around the corner is the Jardins de Càndida Pérez, tucked away in the centre of a classic Eixample-style apartment block. This hidden garden is an example of what designer Ildefons Cerdà dreamed of building for all residents, but only a small number came to fruition.

10

BODEGA 1900
Carrer de Tamarit, 91
933 25 26 59
bodega1900.com
Open Tues–Sat 1–10.30pm
Metro: Paral·lel

With its diminutive size, informal ambience and affordable prices, Bodega 1900 means even travellers on a budget can have an authentic Adrià brothers dining experience. The legendary Adrià brothers are famous for the 'molecular gastronomy' they serve at their many Michelin-starred Barcelona restaurants. Sticking to the principles of the traditional Catalan bodega (wine shop), the menu features cured meats, homemade pickles, preserved shellfish and other delights to nibble on with your vermouth aperitivo (pre-meal drink and snack). Be sure to book a table in advance, as it's a particularly busy spot. Don't miss the Adrià's famous liquid olive 'spheres', a dish that became an icon of the three-Michelin-starred (and five times world's best restaurant) elBulli, which catapulted the two chefs to gastronomic stardom.

The **Escalera de Incendios** (Carrer Parlament, 26, escaleradeincendios.com), or 'fire escape ladder', gallery runs regular exhibitions and is a great place to meet and buy pieces directly from local artists, especially if you're into more progressive, avant-garde art. Head to **Renoir Floridablanca** (Carrer de Floridablanca, 135, cinesrenoir.com) to watch arthouse films and the latest blockbusters in English – the perfect way to escape the summer heat for a few hours.

Enjoy a dose of culture, history and beery goodness at **Fàbrica Moritz** (Ronda de Sant Antoni, 39–41, moritz.com), Barcelona's oldest brewery. It's housed in the original building, which dates back to 1864 and displays the original equipment the company used to get the now-iconic brand off the ground.

Keep an eye out for the area's colourful street art. One of Barcelona's most famous pieces is the hot-air balloon sprayed on the **La Carbonería** ('the coal-house') building, an abandoned house located at the crossroads of Carrer del Comte d'Urgell and Carrer de Floridablanca.

To make sure you eat all the right things in all the right places, join one of the **Barcelona Eat Local food tours** (barcelonaeatlocal.com) and enjoy an indulgent day out at some the area's culinary gems.

Alex Lazarowicz is owner and brewer at Barna Brew (*see* p. 210), a brewpub offering creative tapas and Belgian-inspired Catalan beers.

Mercat de Sant Antoni (Carrer del Comte d'Urgell): This jewel of Modernist architecture has enjoyed a nine-year, multi-million euro renovation, opened to the public in March 2018. The market will retake its place as the cultural centrepiece of Sant Antoni, with food stalls battling for attention with archaeological findings. If you pass by on a Sunday you'll also see the Mercat Domenical de Sant Antoni, a flea market trading old books and comics. I love watching the father–son trading of football stickers that takes place on the margins.

Cafes Roure (Carrer del Comte Borrell, 48): Head to this old-world coffee shop and pick up a bag of freshly ground beans to take home with you. You can also sit at the bar and enjoy a cup of coffee with the locals. Try a cigalo amb rom (espresso with rum, whiskey or baileys) to see why the regulars all have such big grins on their faces.

Bodega d'En Rafel (Carrer de Manso, 52): Tucked away on Carrer de Manso by Mercat de Sant Antoni, this is a proper Spanish-style bodega (wine shop) where the locals hang out from early in the afternoon. The wine and vermouth is poured straight from the barrels, and there's a good beer offering too.

Bodega Sepulveda (Carrer de Sepúlveda, 173): Don't let the name fool you: this is more than just another old bodega (wine shop). It has an extensive menu featuring high-quality meat and fish, and Catalan classics. My favourites are the coques de tonyina (there is a basic and a spicy version) and the courgette carpaccio with cod.

ARRIVING BY AIR

Barcelona El Prat (BCN) is the city's major international airport located 12 kilometres (7.5 miles) south-west of the city centre. There are two terminals, T1 and T2, with a free shuttle bus running between them.

The **Renfe train** service runs from T2 to the city centre, with two trains per hour. There's only one platform and one route into the city, which means you don't have to worry about getting on the wrong train. English-speaking staff are on duty to help new arrivals purchase the right tickets to get to their destinations. At 9.95€, the cost-effective T10 travel ticket is valid for 10 journeys on Barcelona's train, metro and bus services. The journey to the city centre takes 25 to 30 minutes, with stops at Barcelona Sants, Passeig de Gràcia (the most central) and Clot. You can connect with the metro system at all of these stations.

The blue **Aerobus** has buses running from the airport's T1 and T2 terminals every 5 to 10 minutes. Tickets cost 5.90€ one way or 10.20€ return (children under four travel for free) – you can buy tickets directly from the bus driver. The journey takes the same amount of time as the train (25 to 30 minutes), but generally works out to be quicker as they run so much more frequently. The Aerobus stops at Plaça Espanya, Gran Via-Urgell, Plaça Universitat and Plaça Catalunya (City Centre).

There's a night bus for late arrivals, although it is painfully slow. If you are arriving late, it might be better to jump in a taxi, which will cost around 30 to 35€ and take 20 to 25 minutes.

WI-FI

Most cafes and bars in Barcelona offer complimentary wi-fi (pronounced 'wee-fee'). The city also offers free wi-fi in 633 public spaces, including parks, squares and libraries. You can find your nearest wi-fi zone at ajuntament. barcelona.cat/barcelonawifi/en. You will also find many opportunities to buy a SIM card for your phone, whether at the airport or Sants train station on arrival, or at the many phone/media stores throughout the city. Orange, Vodafone, Movistar and Yoigo are the leading phone companies and most have English-speaking staff. Expect to pay around 10-20€ for 1GB of data and enough call minutes to last a week or two.

PUBLIC HOLIDAYS

Spain takes its public holidays extremely seriously, and Barcelona also celebrates additional Catalan holidays. If the holiday lands on, say, a Tuesday, Barcelonians will often take off the Monday as well, referring to it as a puente (bridge). There are 16 official public holidays in Barcelona; some dates shift from year to year: New Year's Day (1 January); Epiphany, or 'Three Kings' as it's known locally (6 January); Good Friday (April); Easter Monday (April); Labour Day (1 May); Whit Monday (5 June); Saint John's Day (24 June); The Assumption (15 August); Catalan National Day (11 September); La Mercè (25 September); Spanish National Holiday (12 October); All Saints' Day (1 November); Constitution Day (6 December); The Immaculate Conception (8 December); Christmas Day (25 December); Boxing Day (26 December).

TOURIST INFORMATION

There are a number of tourist information points located throughout Barcelona, but the main office is located in Plaça de Catalunya (literally underneath it). Here you can find all the information and advice you might need, and book tickets for tours and attractions.

Plaça de Catalunya, 17-S
932 85 38 34
Open Mon–Sun 8.30am–9pm
See all tourist office locations on the Barcelona Turisme website (barcelonaturisme.com/wv3/en/page/38/tourist-information-points.html).

GETTING AROUND

Barcelona's extensive and affordable public transport network is made up of the TMB bus and metro (subway) services. Most people opt for the metro because it is faster and easier to navigate than the bus system.

The T10 travel ticket priced at 9.95€ for 10 journeys, is a cost-effective option for using the train, bus and metro. Hola BCN! travel cards offer unlimited travel by train, bus and metro for two, three, four or five days and are priced at 14.50€, 21.20€, 27.50€ and 33.70€ respectively. Tickets can be purchased at any metro station.

Walking

Barcelona is a walking city – it's possible to explore almost all of it on foot. Walking can also be quicker than taking public transport, especially during festival periods when most of the roads in the city centre are dominated by pedestrians. When giving directions, many longtime Barcelona residents will refer to the sea or the mountain to help with orientation.

No matter where you are in the city, even in the Old Town, you can normally see the mountains that box the city in from behind, which means you can always work out which way it is to the beach (typically downhill). If you do get lost in the Old Town, simply keep an eye out for the maps that point out exactly where you are or pop into the nearest metro station and ask a member of staff for help. You can also ask a local shopkeeper for directions to a familiar area, such as La Rambla or Plaça de Catalunya. Most of the neighbourhoods set outside of the Old Town are laid out in a grid system, which makes them easy to navigate.

Metro

Barcelona's metro system runs Sun–Thurs 5–12am, Fri 5–2am and all night on Saturdays. The metro also runs all night during holidays, but with fewer trains per hour. Lines are colour-coded and numbered, with plenty of easy-to-read signage. A free travel app is available from the TMB website (tmb.cat/en/barcelona/applications-downloads).

Bus

Barcelona's TMB bus service runs efficiently and covers the entire city. Route maps and schedules can be found on the official website (tmb.cat/en/barcelona/buses/lines).

There is also a night bus service (Nit Bus), which runs from around 12–6am. Night buses depart from Barcelona's Plaça de Catalunya – routes and schedules can be found at the bus stops. The N17 (Terminal 1) and N16 (Terminal 2) night buses run from Plaça de Catalunya to the airport.

Cycling

Barcelona is an extremely bike-friendly city, with some 200 kilometres (124 miles) of dedicated cycle lanes. Cyclists can access much of the city and a number of scenic routes, including the 6 kilometre (3.7 mile) beachfront boardwalk that traces the city's entire coastline.

There are countless bike rental companies located in convenient locations throughout Barcelona, particularly in the Old Town and near Barceloneta beach. Bikes can be hired by the hour, day or week, with prices starting at just a few euros. Bike tours are also a great way to see more of the city in less time. Check out Bamboo Bike Tours (bamboobiketour.com) and Steel Donkey Bike Tours (steeldonkeybiketours.com).

Taxi

Barcelona's taxis are very affordable by European standards and are generally easy to flag down. Official Barcelona taxis are yellow and black with a green light on the roof showing availability.

Rates are displayed on a screen inside the taxi. Tipping is welcomed, but not expected. If you would like to leave a tip, then 5 to 10 per cent of the fare is enough.

LOCAL LINGO

Barcelona is a city of two official languages: Spanish (Castilian) and Catalan (Català). Catalan was banned entirely from 1939 to 1975 during Franco's dictatorship, but today around 50 to 60 per cent of the city's population speaks it. It's rare that you will encounter someone who speaks Catalan and not Spanish, but you will get extra points for using a few Catalan words about town.

Hola (Spanish and Catalan, pronounced *or-la*) = hello

Buenas dias (Spanish, pronounced *bwen-ass dee-ass*), **bon dia** (Catalan, pronounced *bon dee-ah*) = good day

Hadios (Spanish, pronounced *ah-dee-os*), **adeu** (Catalan, pronounced *ah-day-oo*) = goodbye

Perdón (Spanish, pronounced *per-don*), **perdoni** (Catalan, pronunce *per-don-ee*) = excuse me

La cuenta por favor (Spanish, pronounced *la kwenta por-fa-vor*), **el compte si us plau** (Catalan, pronounced *el comp-the sees plow*) = Can I have the check please.

¿Habla inglés? (Spanish, pronounced *ah-bla ing-les*), **¿parles anglès?** (Catalan, pronounced *parcels ang-les*) = Do you speak English?

¿Cuánto cuesta? (Spanish, pronounced *kwan-tow kwes-ta*), **¿quant costa?** (Catalan, pronounced *want costa?*) = How much is it?

Calle (Spanish, pronounced *kaiy-eh*), **carrer** (Catalan, pronounced *ca-rrer*) = street. In Barcelona, all street signs are displayed in Catalan.

Por favor (Spanish, pronounced *por-fa-vor*) **si us plau** (Catalan, pronounced *sees-plow*) = please.

Gracias (Spanish, pronounced *grass-y-ass* or *grath-y-ass*), **merci** (Catalan, pronounced *mare-see*) = thank you

Vale (Spanish, pronounced *bah-lee*) = OK. Used a great deal in Spanish.

ETIQUETTE AND LIFESTYLE

Barcelonians are generally polite and welcoming people, and traditional greetings are widely appreciated. Whether entering a shop, taxi, cafe or restaurant, it's always worth opening with a polite 'hola, buenas dias' (hello, good day) and ending with 'gracias' (thank you). To show respect for the local Catalan language, you can also start with 'bon dia' (good day) and leave with 'adéu' (goodbye). Always try to use whatever Spanish/Catalan you know, but don't be surprised if you are answered in English.

Eating out

As with most European cities, Barcelona respects its set meal times. Many places will open for lunch and close until dinner, while more casual cafes and restaurants will remain open throughout the day.

Though you will find plenty of breakfast options in the city centre, it is not considered as important a meal as in other parts of the world. A light breakfast of cafe con leche (coffee with milk) and a small pastry is typically eaten from 8 to 10am, though you might spot locals enjoying a glass of wine or a small beer. A similar media mañana (mid-morning breakfast) is eaten from 11am to 12pm. Brunch is a relatively new concept in Barcelona (and Spain in general), but you will find many trendy options throughout the city offering American-style dishes.

Those with time on their hands might enjoy an aperitivo of vermouth and preserved shellfish – cockles, mussels, bacalao – at midday to open the palate and work up an appetite for lunch.

Lunch is unquestionably the most important meal of the day in Spain, typically eaten from 1.30 to 3.30pm. During the weekdays, many restaurants will offer a set menú del dia (menu of the day), which typically includes three courses, bread and a drink. They are typically aimed at busy locals and offer excellent quality and value for money. Most places, even if they're known for their set menus, will have a separate menu that can be ordered a la carte. Lunch is the only time the Spanish eat paella, as they deem it to be far too heavy to be eaten for dinner. The best paella in Barcelona will always be served at lunchtime, as restaurants know it's only tourists who order it for dinner.

Around 5 or 6pm, many locals will go for an afternoon merienda (snack). This is typically something sweet with a coffee, perhaps a pastry or churros with melted chocolate. Savoury meriendas might include bocadillos (sandwiches) filled with quality sliced ham or a wedge of tortilla (potato omelette).

Dinner starts late in Spain – rarely before 9pm – with some sitting down to eat as late as 11pm. Meal sizes are generally smaller than those eaten at lunch, with many opting for a few small tapas to share with friends and loved ones. But as a large and cosmopolitan city, you will find all sorts of dining options for dinner at all hours of the evening. No one will be in any way offended should you order a large meal (or even a paella).

The level of service varies greatly from venue to venue, as does the level of English spoken. Staff at older, more traditional restaurants in the city centre may take a little while to bring you a menu and take your order, a result of the laid-back approach to dining (and life in general) here.

It is not customary in Spain to request changes to certain dishes, although staff will try to oblige you if you ask politely. Just don't be too surprised if the dish arrives without your requested changes. Restaurants are becoming more accustomed to serving customers with food intolerances and will typically be able to make recommendations or even adapt certain dishes.

Getting the bill may require multiple requests. The upside is that you rarely feel like you are being rushed out the door to make way for incoming diners. Tipping is not obligatory, although most locals will round up on the bill or leave 5 to 10 per cent. A service charge is sometimes included. Also be aware that many restaurants charge a surcharge of up to 15 per cent for dining on their highly coveted outdoor terraces.

Coffee

Tomando un cafe (taking a coffee) is a huge part of the Spanish way of life. The ritual isn't simply about drinking a coffee, but also about taking a moment to relax and connect with others, perhaps at a lively cafe or on a sunny terrace. As such, takeaway coffee is almost unheard of in Spain, as it doesn't allow the drinker to indulge fully in the experience.

Traditional bars and cafes will serve a basic blend of beans at a very low price and tend to use UHT pasteurized milk instead of fresh milk. Aficionados will find premium-quality coffee made with fresh milk and locally roasted beans at Barcelona's many third-wave coffee shops, albeit at significantly higher prices. These places will also serve alternative milk varieties, such as almond milk and soy milk, which are all but impossible to find in traditional Spanish cafes.

You'll want to be familiar with traditional Spanish coffee terminology, including:

Un cafe con leche (Spanish, pronounced *oon cafe con le-chay*): steamed milk with a shot of espresso (similar to a latte)

Un americano (Spanish, pronounced *oon Americano*): espresso topped up with boiling water, served black or with a drop of milk (similar to a long black/Americano)

Un cafe solo (Spanish, pronounced *oon cafe solo*): a small, intense shot of black espresso

Un cortado (Spanish, pronounced *oon cor-tah-do*): the same as a cafe solo but with a splash of hot milk

Un cafe con hielo (Spanish, pronounced *oon cafe con ee-yellow*): coffee served in a cup alongside a glass with ice. Pour it over the ice and let it cool before drinking

Un carajillo (Spanish, pronounced *oon cara-hee-oh*): a shot of espresso served with either rum, whisky or brandy

INDEX

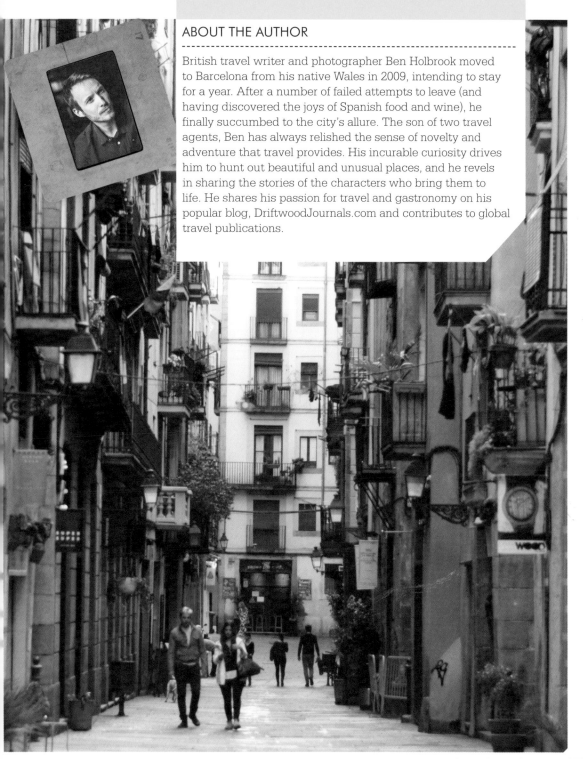

ABOUT THE AUTHOR

British travel writer and photographer Ben Holbrook moved to Barcelona from his native Wales in 2009, intending to stay for a year. After a number of failed attempts to leave (and having discovered the joys of Spanish food and wine), he finally succumbed to the city's allure. The son of two travel agents, Ben has always relished the sense of novelty and adventure that travel provides. His incurable curiosity drives him to hunt out beautiful and unusual places, and he revels in sharing the stories of the characters who bring them to life. He shares his passion for travel and gastronomy on his popular blog, DriftwoodJournals.com and contributes to global travel publications.

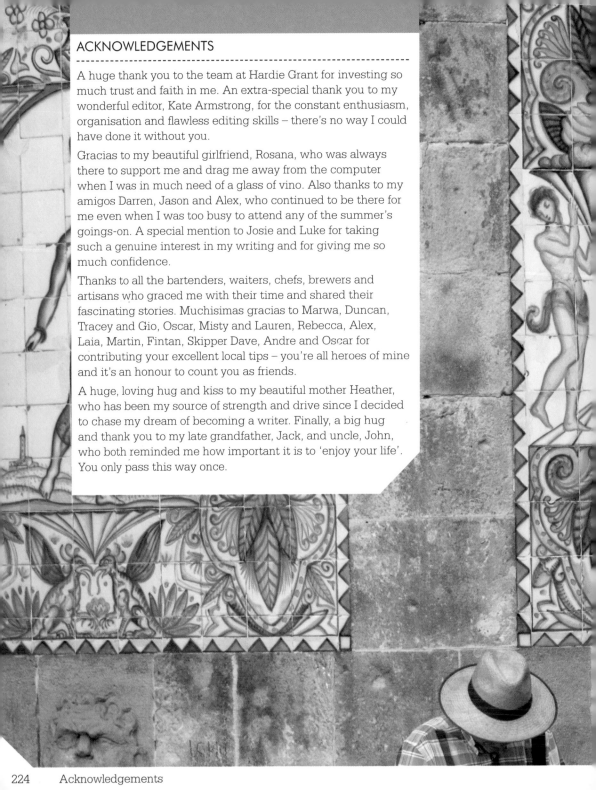

ACKNOWLEDGEMENTS

A huge thank you to the team at Hardie Grant for investing so much trust and faith in me. An extra-special thank you to my wonderful editor, Kate Armstrong, for the constant enthusiasm, organisation and flawless editing skills – there's no way I could have done it without you.

Gracias to my beautiful girlfriend, Rosana, who was always there to support me and drag me away from the computer when I was in much need of a glass of vino. Also thanks to my amigos Darren, Jason and Alex, who continued to be there for me even when I was too busy to attend any of the summer's goings-on. A special mention to Josie and Luke for taking such a genuine interest in my writing and for giving me so much confidence.

Thanks to all the bartenders, waiters, chefs, brewers and artisans who graced me with their time and shared their fascinating stories. Muchisimas gracias to Marwa, Duncan, Tracey and Gio, Oscar, Misty and Lauren, Rebecca, Alex, Laia, Martin, Fintan, Skipper Dave, Andre and Oscar for contributing your excellent local tips – you're all heroes of mine and it's an honour to count you as friends.

A huge, loving hug and kiss to my beautiful mother Heather, who has been my source of strength and drive since I decided to chase my dream of becoming a writer. Finally, a big hug and thank you to my late grandfather, Jack, and uncle, John, who both reminded me how important it is to 'enjoy your life'. You only pass this way once.

Photography credits

All images are © Ben Holbrook, except for the following (letters indicate where multiple images appear on a page, from top to bottom, left to right):

ii–iii courtesy of Eldiset; 003 courtesy of Cereria Subirà; 004 (a) courtesy of Sombrería Obach, (b) courtesy of Toni Pons; 005 (c & e) courtesy of Sombrería Obach, (a, b, d & f) courtesy of Toni Pons; 006–007 courtesy of It Reminds Me Of Something; 010–011 courtesy of La Colmena; 018–019 courtesy of Ocaña; 021 Daniela Giannangeli; 022 courtesy of Sidecar; 023 (a) courtesy of Marula Café, (b & c) courtesy of Sidecar; 025 courtesy of Swiit; 028–029 courtesy of Les Topettes; 032–033 courtesy of Grey Street; 035 courtesy of Wilde Sunglasses; 036 (a) Rey Perezoso, (b) courtesy of Rocambolesc; 037 (a) courtesy of Rocambolesc, (b & c) courtesy of Granja M. Viader; 038–039 courtesy of Carvelle; 045 (a) courtesy of Boadas Cocktails; 047 courtesy of Rebecca McNally Coleman; 050 courtesy of Nu Sabates; 051 courtesy of Ici Et Là; 052 courtesy of Coquette; 054 (a) courtesy of Ivori, (b) courtesy of Natalie Capell Atelier de Moda; 055 (a & b courtesy of Natalie Capell Atelier de Moda), (c) courtesy of Ivori; 056 courtesy of La Tercera; 062–063 courtesy of NAP; 065 courtesy of Eldiset; 068 (a) courtesy of Antic Teatre; 069 (a, d & e) courtesy of Antic Teatre; 071 Fintan Kerr; 078–079 courtesy of Blacklab Brewhouse & Kitchen; 81 courtesy of Bacoa; 082–083 courtesy of Salt Beach Club; 084–085 courtesy of Eclipse Skybar; 089 David Baird; 098–099 courtesy of Els Pescadors; 100–101 courtesy of Madame George; 102–103 Sergio Ävila; 104 courtesy of Niu Espai Artístic; 105 courtesy of Razzmatazz; 107 Duncan Rhodes; 112 (b), 113 (c) courtesy of Santa Eulalia; 116 courtesy of Monvinic; 119 Marwa Preston; 122 courtesy of The Avant; 125 courtesy of Delacrem; 135 Oscar Fuentes Loyola; 144–145 Marta Balcells; 146 (b) Lauren Aloise; 151 Misty Barker; 160 courtesy of Tram-Tram; 163 courtesy of The Sutton Club; 165 courtesy of Laia Martinell; courtesy of Martinez; 174–175 courtesy of Addis Abeba; 177 (b) Jorge Franganillo; 178–179 La Terrrazza; 181 courtesy of Martin Ebner; 184 courtesy of Brummell Souvenir Shop; 185 courtesy of Spice Café; 188–189 courtesy of The Tatami Room; 193 (b) courtesy of Malamén; 194 (a) courtesy of El Molino; 197 courtesy of Andre Arriaza; 200–201 courtesy of Trait Store; 202 courtesy of El Recibidor; 204-205 courtesy of La Donuteria; 206 courtesy of The Juice House; 208–209 courtesy of Jovani & Vins; 210 (b) courtesy of Tarannà Cafè, 211 (b) courtesy of Tarannà Cafè; 213 courtesy of Bodega 1900.

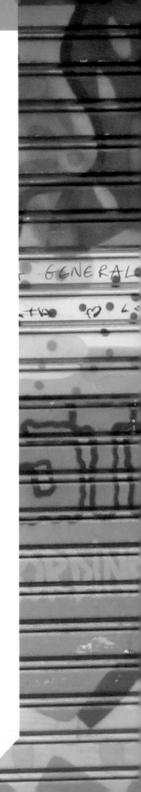

Published in 2018 by Hardie Grant Travel, a division of Hardie Grant Publishing

Hardie Grant Travel (Melbourne)
Building 1, 658 Church Street
Richmond, Victoria 3121

Hardie Grant Travel (Sydney)
Level 7, 45 Jones Street
Ultimo, NSW 2007

hardiegranttravel.com

A Cataloguing-in-Publication entry is available from the catalogue of the National Library of Australia at www.nla.gov.au

Barcelona Precincts
ISBN 9781741175554

10 9 8 7 6 5 4 3 2 1

Publisher
Melissa Kayser

Project editor
Kate Armstrong, Megan Cuthbert

Proofreader
Susan Paterson

Cartographers
Bruce McGurty, Emily Maffei

Design and Illustrations
Michelle Mackintosh

Typesetting
Megan Ellis

Index
Max McMaster

Prepress
Megan Ellis and Splitting Image Colour Studio

Printed and bound in China by 1010 Printing International Limited

A free digital download of the text and maps from this book is available at: https://goo.gl/Vi9HmG Just make sure to have this book handy, so you can answer some questions as proof of purchase.